MW01181284

THE SUNNY SIDE OF COOKING

Solar cooking and other ecologically friendly
cooking methods for the 21st century

By Lisa Rayner

The Sunny Side of Cooking:
Solar cooking and other ecologically friendly
cooking methods for the 21st century
First edition, Copyright (c) 2007 Lisa Rayner

ISBN 978-0-9800608-0-5

Published and distributed by Lifeweaver LLC

P.O. Box 22324
Flagstaff, AZ 86002
lisa@LisaRayner.com
www.LisaRayner.com

HATHOR FONT
Copyright (c) Jeni Pleskow
Fonts by Jeni
http://rois.org/fonts.html
rois@iconoclast.org

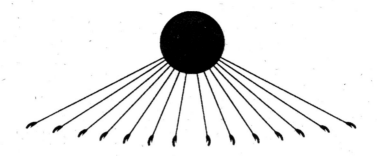

TABLE OF CONTENTS

Introduction

Solar cooking—the sustainable solution

What if there was a method of cooking that was low cost, powered by sunlight, non-polluting, and easy to do even in college dorms, on apartment balconies and at off-the-grid locations? There is: solar cooking.

At the dawn of the 21st century, the need for sustainable cooking solutions is great: fossil fuel-caused global warming and climate change; rising energy costs due to the end of cheap oil and political instability in petroleum exporting regions; fossil fuel pollution such as acid rain and mercury contamination from burning coal; and deforestation and resulting soil erosion and desertification (globally, most firewood is cut down for cooking).

I first learned about the revolutionary idea of permaculture two decades ago. Permaculture, which means both "permanent agriculture" and "permanent culture," is a holistic science of design based on the principles of ecology. One of permaculture's core design principles is that just like a tree or other natural object, each element in a holistic design system should perform many functions. Solar cooking embodies this principle by solving multiple problems.

I have eaten a vegan diet (no animal products) for 20 years, and have been vegetarian even longer. I have been a solar cook for 12 years. I teach vegetarian and solar cooking workshops in northern Arizona. I have found the few existing solar cookbooks to be limited in the variety of cooking techniques they explore. It is possible to do everything from simmering to braising, steaming, sautéing, baking, roasting, toasting, grilling and more in a solar cooker.

I am grateful to have learned much about solar cooking directly from solar cooker inventor and solar cooking pioneer Barbara Prosser Kerr, who lives less than a two-hour drive from me in Taylor, Arizona. Kerr has loaned me several of her solar cookers for use in my solar cooking workshops. Kerr's collaborator, solar engineer James Scott, has provided excellent technical information on the design and functioning of solar cookers.

The Sunny Side of Cooking is designed to be simple, straightforward and, above all, practical. Part I describes the basic principles of solar cooking and helps you decide which type of solar cooker will best meet your needs. Part II provides specific cooking instructions for grains, beans, pasta, vegetables, fruit, soups, casseroles, breads, pies, cakes, cookies, tofu, tempeh, seitan and more. It also includes information on USDA-approved solar canning techniques, water pasteurization, and even using your solar cooker to cool food and make ice (at night!).

While solar cooking is clearly the most ecological way to cook in sunny climates because it requires no fuel, other fuel-efficient methods like fireless cooking, pressure cooking, earth ovens, and wood stoves are important adjuncts to solar cooking. Together, these methods create a year-round sustainable cooking system that works in all climates. Part III discusses these complementary cooking methods.

The Appendix in Part IV lists numerous Web sites, books, organizations and other resource materials that can help you transition to a sustainable way of cooking.

Praise for *The Sunny Side of Cooking*

"This new solar cookbook by Lisa Rayner is beautifully
detailed and informative. I highly recommend it
both for beginners and experienced solar cooks who may
pick up some useful variations and additional uses.
Her recipes make one's mouth water just reading them!
I know you are in for a lot of pleasure as you explore how
your solar cooker fits into your household routine
and the variety of foods it can bring to perfection.
Go for it!"

— Barbara Prosser Kerr
Solar cooking pioneer
Co-inventor of the Kerr-Cole EcoCooker™
Kerr-Cole Sustainable Living Center, Taylor, AZ

"For as long as I have been associated with Barbara
she has been on the lookout for persons to carry forward
the knowledge she has accrued over the years. Especially
she has wished to foster persons to teach folks in their
community to solar cook and to apply the allied practices
such as fireless cooking and efficient fuel-wood cooking.
You are a godsend to her, for not only are you teaching
solar cooking classes but you are also adding to the body
of knowledge. Furthermore you are promulgating
it widely by publishing this book on the subject.
I hope the book will inspire others to also become teachers.
We are most grateful that you have taken such an active
role in the promotion of these methods.
I find this text to be very clearly written, well organized,
complete and succinct. But I think you already know this.
Bravo for a thorough and easily understood
coverage of the essential topics!"

— James Scott
Solar engineer
Kerr-Cole Sustainable Living Center, Snowflake, AZ

PART I

The basics of solar cooking

A solar cooker collects sunlight
and transforms it into heat.
Solar cookers come in a variety
of designs suited for every climate, budget,
living situation, skill level and cooking need.
Once you get in the habit of using a solar
cooker, you'll discover that solar cooking
is easier and more relaxed than
other forms of cooking.

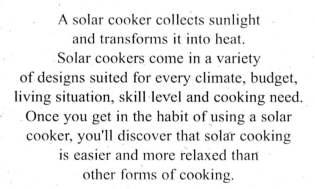

CHAPTER ONE
Anyone can be a solar cook

Solar cooking is possible in most areas of the world, even in far northern latitudes such as Norway. Counterintuitively, the mid-latitudes frequently have more consistent sun exposure than the tropics, which are frequently cloudy. Sunny, arid regions have the best year-round solar cooking conditions.

You can use a solar cooker if:

◉ You live between 60° north and south of the equator, from mid-Canada and Russia south to the entire continents of South America, Africa and Australia.
◉ Between 60° and 40° latitude, it is possible to solar cook during spring, summer and fall.
◉ South of 40° (Salt Lake City, UT; Newark, NJ) year-round solar cooking is possible. In North America, the Southwest has the highest intensity of solar radiation. However, even cloudy places like the Pacific Northwest and New England are suitable for solar cooking part of the year.
◉ You have a sunny spot unobstructed by shade for at least 3 hours per day.

Solar cooking is even possible if:

◉ You live in an apartment or townhome.
◉ You are away at work all day.
◉ Traveling or backpacking!

Average annual solar radiation in the continental United States
Direct beam radiation with parabolic collectors tracking the sun in both
azimuth (east-west directionality) and elevation. The Southwest receives 5–10
kilowatts/m²/day. Small areas in the Pacific Northwest and Great Lakes
receive only 2–3 kWh/m²/day. National Renewable Resource Data Center.

My experience

A friend of mine had for many years a huge mirrored, multiple reflector Solar
Chef™ on wheels (see Chapter Two). I was always envious of the beautiful
design, large interior size, high
temperatures and ease of portability.

My story is much simpler. For my
first few years of solar cooking,
I lived in a second floor apartment. I would carry my cardboard cooker, a used CooKit™
(pictured) purchased for $10, downstairs
and set it up against the south facing wall of my
apartment building, protected from stray dogs by an
impenetrable hedge of junipers. I was able to look out my
bedroom window at the cooker to keep an eye on it.

Since 1999, I have lived in a townhome with a south-facing balcony. My
solar cooker is now a Sun Oven™ with four reflectors (see picture on next
page). Flagstaff, Arizona is a very windy place, especially during the spring
dry season. The wind funnels through my townhome complex pretty fierce-
ly. My Sun Oven™ is set up on a camping table on top of a homemade Lazy-

Susan constructed out of plywood. (The Lazy Susan makes it easy to rotate the oven to track the sun.) The oven is attached to the Lazy Susan with small bungee cords on all four corners. The Lazy Susan is attached to the table with large utility clips. The table is attached to the balcony with large bungee cords. During an especially windy day, the reflectors flap like the sails of a clipper ship on the high seas. No matter — it works! I transport the cooker, which has fold-up reflectors, in a Burley™ bicycle trailer when I give solar cooking demonstrations.

Flagstaff is at 37° north latitude and 7,000 feet elevation (2,133 meters). My Sun Oven™ hovers between 300–325°F/149–163°C on clear, sunny days, and 200–250°F/93–121°C on partly cloudy days. I use it on an almost daily basis. Luckily for me, I live in a sunny, high desert environment optimum for solar cooking. However, even on partly cloudy winter days and during the Southwest's rainy summer Monsoon season, when towering thunderheads build up during the afternoon, I use my oven to cook foods that don't require high temperatures or long cooking times.

Awareness and flexibility are key

It's truly amazing how much food you can cook in a solar cooker. My Sun Oven™ has interior dimensions of 14" x 14", large enough for a 9" x 13" casserole dish or a large stock pot. My husband and I are a family of two. However, I could easily cook for a family of six with the Sun Oven™. While I am vegan, it is even possible to cook a large turkey in a solar cooker.

Place your cooker in an easy-to-use location. It is ideal to store the cooker outdoors right where it will be used. Protect it from moisture and wind with a waterproof cover (I use a barbeque grill tarp).

The key to successful solar cooking is forethought and planning. Modern cooking appliances have made it easy for those of us in industrialized countries to forget about food until we feel hungry. When we are ready to eat, heating prepared foods or cooking a simple meal is nearly instantaneous. To be honest, it takes some effort to retrain yourself to be aware of the weather conditions and the day's cooking needs. When I was a novice solar cook, I often forget to put food in my solar cooker until it was too late.

Permaculture designers have a saying: "The problem is the solution." A friend says, "Think of (solar cooking) as the meditative work of a simpler life: put the pot of water in the solar oven as soon as the sun is up (or as soon as you wake up, if the sun rises earlier than you do!), and you can have your morning cup by the time you have retrieved the paper. If you have a solar parabolic reflector, your water will boil in no time at all." Once you begin to make the switch, the satisfaction of knowing that the sun is cooking your food will act as reinforcement to your developing awareness. Opening up a pot of hot, steaming solar stew is the ultimate encouragement to solar cooking.

Once you get into the swing of things, it's easy to cook a succession of dishes throughout the day. I work at home. A typical day begins with opening up my Sun Oven™ as soon as I get up (8–9 a.m.). My first dish might be solar pancakes, which take about an hour. Next, I'll put in a casserole for lunch or some type of baked dessert, such as fruit cobbler. In the afternoon, I'll throw in a pot of grains, polenta or potatoes for dinner. On days when I have lots of leftovers to eat, I'll use the cooker to heat the leftovers or make soup stock, herbal tea or cook a batch of beans to divide and freeze for later use. My house begins to shade my cooker sometime between 3–5 p.m. depending on the time of year; because I don't have a yard, that's it for the day.

Anyone can be a solar cook 5

Solar food dryers

Solar cookers do not make good food dryers, partly because of their small size, partly because they are so moist, and partly because the temperature is usually too high. Drying is best done between 100–140°F/38–60°C. Some solar dryers look similar to a solar cooker, but are thinner and flatter; a venting system allows hot air to evaporate the moisture out of the food. Some designs keep the drying food out of direct sunlight and use the sun to power a sophisticated downdraft venting system. See the appendix for a list of solar drying books, articles and plans.

A brief history of solar cooking

Solar cooking has been practiced for thousands of years. The first form involved placing food directly onto rocks heated by the sun. For instance, Jewish Essenes living along the shores of the Dead Sea in the Second Century B.C. dried thin wafers of sprouted grains, today known as Essene bread, using this technique. The Greeks, Romans, Incas and Aztecs used curved parabolic mirrors to concentrate sunlight to produce high heat.

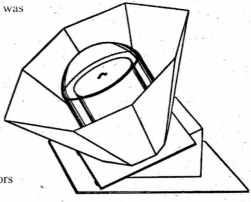

The first modern solar cooker was invented by Swiss naturalist Horace de Saussure in 1767. Saussure reported that his "hot box," constructed of several nested clear glass boxes, poached fruit at a temperature of 190°F/88°C. In 1878, inventor W. A. Adam patented a very modern-looking, nearly parabolic box cooker with eight reflectors called the "Adams Solar Cooking Apparatus" that looks remarkably like the Solar Chef™.

Adams Solar Cooking Apparatus

In the 1950s, the United Nations began sponsoring studies of solar cookers to help people in developing countries. In 1976 during the OPEC oil embargo, Arizona environmentalists Barbara Kerr and Sherry Cole introduced the first commercial solar box oven, the cardboard, single reflector

EcoCooker™. Today, knowledge of the twin ecological threats of global warming and peak oil has spawned a new interest in solar cooking.

International nonprofit organizations such as Solar Cookers International are working to introduce solar cookers to poor and deforested areas of Africa, Asia and Latin America, including war-torn Afganistan and the Darfur region of Sudan. Hundreds of thousands of solar cookers are in use around the world, used for everything from cooking and water pasteurization to medical disinifection and sterilization. SCI also sponsors two Web sites: the Solar Cooking Archive and Solar Cooking Wiki, as well as a printed newsletter and an international solar cooking and pasteurization conference (see Appendix).

Building community through solar cooking

Educate others and build community by bringing a solar cooker to your place of work, school, church, community garden, nature center, or neighborhood park. Host a solar cook-off or potluck. Consider demonstrating multiple cooker designs, or building a community-sized oven to be shared by your neighbors.

CHAPTER TWO
Select the right solar cooker for you

A solar cooker collects sunlight and transforms it into heat. Depending on the cooker design and weather conditions, solar cooker temperatures range from 180–500°F/82–260°C or higher. Even the smallest and simplest solar cookers can cook simple meals for one or two people.

The power of sunlight

Solar cookers harness visible sunlight in three ways. Some cookers use just one or two of these techniques. Some use all three:

- **A miniature greenhouse** created with glass or plastic glazing, an overturned glass bowl or plastic cooking bag. Short-wave visible sunlight enters through the glazing. The inside of this type of cooker is black to absorb the light. The light transforms into longer-wavelength, infrared energy (heat) that cannot pass back out through the glazing, causing the temperature to rise inside the cooker.
- **Sunlight concentration** using reflectors or a foiled cooker interior. The closer to a parabolic shape the reflectors are, the higher the temperature at the point of concentration.
- **Insulation** to retain the collected heat.

At its most basic, a solar cooker simply needs to be aimed towards the sun. If the cooker has moveable reflectors, they should be tilted to capture the most sunlight. Generally speaking, the bigger the cooker, the higher the temperature. Food begins to cook at only 160°F/71°C. The boiling point at sea level is only 212°F/100°C, and lower at higher altitudes (199°F/93°C in Flagstaff, AZ). Even simple solar cookers easily reach these temperatures.

Each variety of cooker has its advantages and drawbacks. Some cookers reach high temperatures but require frequent re-aiming; some cookers are designed for inattentive or absentee cooking. Some cookers are weatherproof; others can't be left out if rain is threatening. Some are very stable in wind; others require a sheltered location. Some can be built cheaply with materials sitting around your home; some commercial models cost several hundred dollars, just like an ordinary electric or gas range. Plans and commercial models for most designs are available at www.solarcooking.org.

There are two main types of solar cookers: box cookers and reflector-only cookers.

Box cookers

Box cookers, also known as solar ovens, are insulated boxes with clear glazing on the sun-facing side. They have black interior walls to absorb sunlight or a foiled interior to reflect sunlight into cooking pots. Both designs function equally well. Box cookers can be outfitted with exterior reflectors to focus additional sunlight into the cooking chamber.

Reflectorless box cooker

Because there are no exterior reflectors, the temperature of a reflectorless box cooker is 220–280°F/ 104–138°C on a sunny day. The glazing is usually slanted to receive the maximum amount of sunlight.

Advantages include stability in wind and the need to re-aim the cooker towards the sun only once or twice a day. Reflectorless box cookers can even be strapped with bungee cords to the top of an RV, truck or van for cooking on the road! The SOS Sport™ is a popular commercial model constructed out of reused plastic soda bottles; the plastic lid lifts off. It comes with two 3-liter graniteware roasters, an oven thermometer and a Water Pasteurization Indicator (see Chapter Eighteen).

Solar wall oven

A solar wall oven is a reflectorless box cooker attached to a south facing building wall. It has a rear access door that goes through the wall, so that the oven can be opened from the inside of the building. Thus, one does not need to go outside to use it. The design was developed by Paul Funk and Barbara Kerr. Kerr's wall oven opens into her kitchen. Kerr leaves the oven "on" (glazing uncovered) all day long, making it as easy to cook with as a microwave. Solar Wall Oven plans are available at http://solarcooking .org/walloven.htm. Commercial models are in development.

Single reflector box cooker

Single reflector box cookers are rectangular boxes with horizontal glazing. The reflector shines sunlight into the oven chamber. The reflector is propped open with a stick and can be adjusted to capture sunlight from different angles. The reflector folds over the oven box for easy storage. The inside of the oven may be black or foiled. In 1976, Barbara Kerr and Sherry Cole invented the first commercial solar box cooker, the cardboard EcoCooker™. Kerr refers to her wooden version as the Patio Cooker™. Wooden versions are very weather resistant and have been used to cook thousands of meals over several decades. Metal versions are also available. Single reflector box cookers reach a maximum temperature of 275–300°F/135–149°C. They are fairly stable in wind and do not need frequent re-aiming because the reflector is able to reflect light into the box from a variety of angles.

Multiple reflector oven

Multiple reflector ovens have four or more reflectors which open up like flower petals to form a crude parabola and slanted glazing. In some models, the reflectors can be folded over the glazing for easy storage. The oven interior may be black or foiled. Some models use the glazing as the door, while others, especially large ones, have a rear access door. Multiple-reflector ovens reach 250–450°F/121–232°C year-round. The Sun Oven™, Heaven's Flame Cooker™ and Solar Chef™ are three popular commerical models. The Sun Oven™ has an adjustable rod attached to the back wall that tilts the oven glazing towards the sun, thus capturing the maximum amount of sunlight year-round from early morning to late afternoon. Sun Ovens International Inc. also manufactures the Villager™, a giant 9-foot high version that reaches 500°F/260°C and can bake hundreds of loaves of bread per day or disinfect medical waste.

Hybrid electric cooker

Hybrid designs combine a box cooker, usually a single reflector model, with an electrical backup heating element and a thermostat that automatically adjusts the electrical output to maintain an even cooking temperature under all weather conditions. One commercial model is the Tulsi-Hybrid™ (www.sunbdcorp.com). The newest design frontier is finding ways to pair hybrid cookers with tube-style skylights such as the Solatube™ for indoor cooking. Hybrid cookers are used in India for medical waste disinfection.

Reflector-only cookers

Do you remember high school geometry? A parabola describe the curvature of the now-ubiquitous satellite dish. Reflector-only cookers have reflectors arranged in a more or less parabolic shape to reflect sunlight directly onto a cooking pot. They have no insulated box.

Parabolic reflector

Also known as solar concentrator cookers, parabolic reflectors, look like satellite dishes. Sunlight is concentrated onto a single point. They reach 500°F/260°C or more very quickly and are used like a stovetop burner (and are just as dangerous!). The disadvantages include instability in wind and the need to re-aint the cooker every 15 minutes because the point of concentration is so small. Because the cooking pot is not insulated, the tempera-ture quickly drops when clouds obscure the sun. A new parabolic design for city- and apartment-dwellers called the "Innovative 'balcony model of solar concentrat-ing cooker'" is included in the proceedings of the Solar Cookers and Food Processing 2006 International Conference. The balcony parabola mounts over the edge of a balcony or parapet wall. It has a retractable hot plate so that the cook does not have to bend over the side of the building to reach the cooking pot.

Funnel Cooker

Funnel cookers have a deep, funnel-shaped reflector that is more elongated than a true parabola. Sunlight concentrates along a vertical line rather than a single point. The funnel is inserted into a box or frame for stability. The cooking pot is placed inside a plastic cooking bag at the bottom of the funnel. Popular models include the cardboard Solar Funnel Cooker™ and a metal design is manufac-tured by Friendly Appropriate Solar Technologies in Los Altos, Calif. (www.fast-solar.com).

Panel cooker

Panel cookers consist of three to five or more reflective panels. A cooking pot is placed inside a plastic oven cooking bag or inverted glass bowl. The front panel is tiltable to capture low-angled or high-angled sunlight. Panel cookers heat food to 200–300°F/93–149°C. They are cheap and simple to construct out of cardboard or wood and foil. They do not require frequent re-aiming. They are very lightweight and can be folded for travel or backpacking. An emergency panel cooker can be constructed out of a reflective foam car windshield shade. The main drawback is the lightweight construction; panel cookers must be weighted down with rocks or bricks in windy locations. The most popular commercial model is Solar Cooking International's cardboard CooKit™ (pictured). Large panel cookers can be used to heat pressure canners (See Chapter Eighteen).

Scheffler-reflector

This innovative design was created by German inventor Wolfgang Scheffler. A parabolic refelctor is flexed to deflect a concentrated beam of light off to the side, where it is directed through an open window onto a hotplate or into a wall oven or Asian tandoor oven.

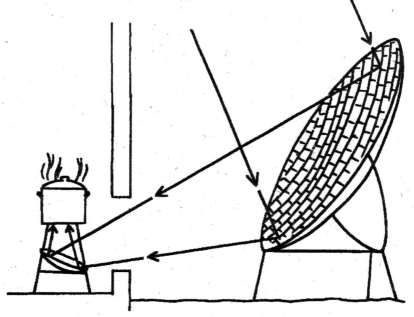

Questions to consider when choosing a solar cooker

Do you live at a northerly latitude? If you live north of the 40° parallel (Philadelphia, Pennsylvania; Denver, Colorado), you need to be able to capture low sun for much of the year. Choose a cooker with tilted glazing, such as the SOS Sport™ or Sun Oven™, or a panel cooker with a nearly vertical back panel.

Do you live at a mid-latitude? Most designs will work for you. Other climatic considerations are more important than latitude.

Do you live near the equator? Choose a cooker designed to capture high-angled sunlight, such as a box cooker with a flat, horizontal top or a parabolic cooker that can be used in the horizontal position. The CooKit™ panel cooker is designed specifically for the equatorial region.

Do you live in a sunny, arid climate? Any solarcooker will work for you. Most of the American West, including high latitude locations like Montana, fit this description.

Do you live in a humid or cloudy climate? This includes sunny, humid places like Florida. Solar ovens with multiple reflectors perform best in hazy or partly cloudy conditions.

Do you live in a windy climate? Choose a sturdy box cooker with few or no reflectors made of plastic, wood or metal, such as the SOS Sport™ or Patio Cooker™. It is possible to use multiple-reflector cookers in windy climates (I do), but you'll have to firmly attach the cooker with bungee cords or tent stakes. Avoid parabolic reflectors; they are particularly vulnerable to wind.

Will you store the cooker outdoors? Wooden and plastic models can be left outdoors year-round (I leave mine on my balcony and cover it with a waterproof barbecue cover). A few models like the SOS Sport™ are weatherproof in wet conditions.

Are you handy with building things and/or low on cash?
Plans are available for many solar cooker designs, including box cookers, panel cookers, funnel cookers and parabolic cookers at www.solarcooking.org. Build your own solar cooker from cardboard, wood, plastic, metal, foil or glass as fits your budget.

Do you prefer hassle-free, inattentive cooking? Choose a box cooker with no reflector or a single reflector, or a panel cooker. With these designs there is no need to frequently re-aim the cooker. Furthermore, food will not burn if left too long.

Do you prefer for your food to cook as fast as possible? Choose a multiple reflector oven or parabolic reflector.

Do you like to cook large volumes of food or multiple dishes at once? Single reflector box cookers usually have lots of floor space, so you can cook several small dishes side-by-side. You'll need a multiple-reflector oven if you want to cook large pots of stew or other foods. Panel cookers are not suitable for cooking large volumes of food.

Do you have a special need for convenience and comfort? Barbara Kerr's Solar Wall Oven™ allows you to solar cook from inside your own kitchen! Scheffler-reflectors™ and thermo-siphon cookers are also designed for indoor cooking.

Do you like to go camping or backpacking or go on road trips? Choose a lightweight, fold-up cardboard panel cooker to bring with you. Another option is to strap a weatherproof reflector-less box cooker such as the SOS Sport™ on top of an RV, camper shell or van with bungee cords for on-the-road cooking.

Do you like to grill and fry foods, preserve foods by canning or do you plan on boiling large volumes of water or other liquids? You'll need a parabolic reflector.

CHAPTER THREE
Solar cooking basics

A t its most basic, a solar cooker simply needs to be aimed towards the sun. The temperature of a solar cooker is directly related to the strength of the sunlight. This chapter explains how to work with the weather to regulate temperatures and cooking times to suit your needs.

Working with the sun

- If your cooker has moveable reflectors or panels, tilt them to capture the most sunlight throughout the day.
- Some cookers like the SOS Sport™ can be flipped in two directions: flatter glazing for when the sun is high in the sky (summer, midday) and steeper glazing for when the sun is low in the sky (early morning, late afternoon and winter). Some box cookers have a rod that can be adjusted to change the tilt of the entire oven in one inch increments; a swinging oven rack keeps the cooking pots level.
- Aim your cooker slightly ahead of the sun's path so that you don't have to re-aim too soon.
- There are two types of solar cooking days: clear and sunny versus hazy or partly cloudy. Solar cookers reach higher temperatures on clear days than on partly cloudy days.
- On days when the sun appears only 15 minutes out of every hour, solar cooking is limited to grains, fruits, vegetables and defrosting or reheating.

- Raw dough and large pots of liquid require full sun.
- Some solar cooks keep a metal baking tray or slab of carbon steel or se soned cast iron on the bottom of the oven, or they cook in cast iron cookware, to retain heat. This method works best during clear, sunny days.
- Higher altitudes experience stronger sunlight than lower altitudes, but the lower boiling point tends to cancel out this advantage.
- Snow can help to reflect more light into your cooker, raising the temperature 25°F/45°C or more.

- Wear a visor and sunglasses to protect yourself from the intense sunlight reflecting off the reflectors.
- Always use potholders when opening a solar cooker and picking up a cooking pot. Solar cookers are nearly as hot as conventional ovens!
- Be careful of steam escaping from an oven or cooking pot when it is opened.

Solar cooking throughout the year

In the mid-latitudes (roughly coinciding with the lower-48 states), the sun travels the following paths across the sky at different times of the year:

- The sun is most directly overhead on the Summer Solstice (June 20–22). It rises in the northeast and sets in the northwest.
- On the Spring and Fall Equinox (March 20–22 and September 20–22), the sun rises due east, travels mid-way across the sky, and sets due west.
- On the Winter Solstice (December 22–22), the sun rises in the southeast, follows a low path across the sky, and sets in the southwest.

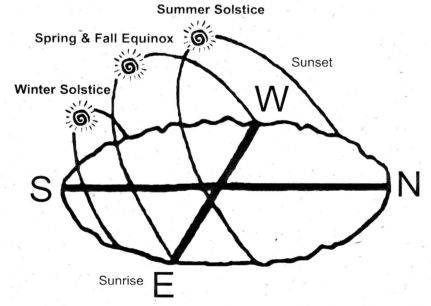

Other weather conditions

- Air temperature has only a moderate effect on oven temperature because insulation traps heat inside a solar cooker very effectively. However, if you store your oven outdoors, it will take longer to heat up on a cold winter morning than on a hot summer day.

- Strong winds carry heat away from the outer surface of the glazing, and directly from the inside of the cooker if the cooker does not have a tight seal. Solar cookers work best when they are used in a wind-sheltered location. On spring days when Flagstaff typically experiences the strongest winds of the year, the temperature in my oven is 50–100°F/10–38°C lower than on very calm days.

Solar cooking times

- Because of weather variables, solar cooking times vary. Food might cook in exactly the same time as on a stovetop or in a conventional oven, or it might take up to three times longer to cook. A solar cooker at 300°F/ 149°C will cook food twice as fast as a solar cooker at only 200°F/93°C.

- Place an oven thermometer inside your solar cooker in an out-of-the-way corner so that you can see the cooking temperature at all times. Commercial models often come with a built-in thermometer.

- Preheating a solar box cooker greatly speeds up the cooking time. If you have been using a box cooker continuously for several hours, it will cook food just about as fast as using conventional methods. Preheating is necessary if using cast iron cookware or if the cooker contains a carbon steel or cast iron slab in the bottom.

- Try to wait the full cooking time before opening the oven, cooking bag or pot so as not to allow hot air to escape. The temperature drops about 50°F/90°C each time the oven or cooking bag is opened. However, don't let this make you too anxious. Check things when you feel you need to, and everything will be OK. Well-insulated box cookers and parabolic reflectors heat up again very quickly.

Solar cookers and food safety

Solar cookers are very safe in terms of preventing the growth of microbes. Disease-producing bacteria and other pathogenic microbes grow fastest between 40°–140°F/4–60°C. To prevent spoilage, cooked food should not be allowed to remain in this danger zone for longer than two hours. Keep food heated above 140°F/60°C or cool it below 40°F/4°C as fast as possible. Solar cookers cook at temperatures between 180°F/82°C and 500°F/260°C. On partly cloudy days, a properly-constructed solar cooker will remain above the danger zone. It is also safe to defrost food in a solar box or panel cooker, even if frozen food is placed in an unheated cooker in the morning and cooked using the absentee cooking method, as long as the midday cooking temperatures are adequate (see next page).

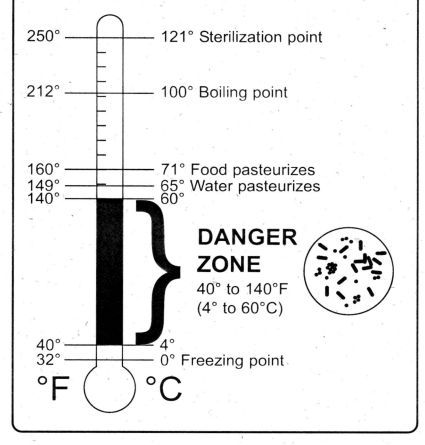

250°	121° Sterilization point
212°	100° Boiling point
160°	71° Food pasteurizes
149°	65° Water pasteurizes
140°	60°

DANGER ZONE
40° to 140°F
(4° to 60°C)

40°	4°
32°	0° Freezing point

°F °C

Regulating the temperature and cooking time

Even if you need to be away from your cooker for several hours or at work all day, food can be cooked and kept warm on your schedule by altering the aim of the cooker. The following techniques work with box cookers and panel cookers, but not reflector-only cookers, which need constant re-aiming.

- If you will be gone up to a few hours, aim the cooker halfway between where the sun is when you leave and where you estimate it will be when you come back. The idea is for the most intense cooking to happen at the mid-point of your absence.
- If you will be gone at work all day and want a warm meal when you get home, position the cooker due south in the morning. Add the pot of food (frozen is OK) and leave. The food will slowly warm up, cook during mid-day, and then gradually cool down.
- You can keep food warm after it is finished cooking by aiming the cooker slightly away from the sun. To prevent the growth of bacteria, make sure the temperature remains above 140°F/60°C (see food safety box on previous page). If the temperature inside the cooker drops too low, aim the cooker more directly towards the sun to raise the temperature.

What if the sun disappears?

- Keep food insulated in a box cooker for up to a couple of hours with a blanket (see Chapter Twenty: Fireless cooking for more information).
- Cast iron cookware and slabs of carbon steel or cast iron will retain heat in a cooker for a while after the sun sets.
- If you are concerned that there may not be enough time to fully cook your food, especially at high latitudes during late fall, winter and early spring, you can speed up the cooking time by bringing the pot to a boil on the stovetop before placing it in the solar cooker.
- If unexpected clouds or haze cut short your solar cooking time, simply switch to another method of cooking. Ovenproof pots can go right into a gas, electric or wood-fired oven. Glass baking dishes are compatible with ovens and microwaves and are sometimes suitable for stovetop simmering. Hot food can also be placed in a fireless cooker to continue cooking.
- When solar cooking is not possible, switch to another ecologically friendly cooking method. That's what Part III: The sustainable kitchen is about.

Speed it up or slow it down

Foods cook fastest when:	Foods cook slowest when:

Foods cook fastest when:

- The solar cooker is preheated for 30 minutes –1 hour.

- The food is cooked in a preheated cast iron pot or on top of a preheated carbon steel or cast iron slab.

- The sky is clear and sunny.

- Cooking is done during midday.

- You are within three months of the Summer Solstice.

- The cooker is re-aimed towards the sun every 30 minutes.

- The food is sliced into small pieces.

- The food is divided into several smaller pots.

Foods cook slowest when:

- Food is placed in an unheated cooker, especially on a cold morning if you store your cooker outdoors.

- Food is placed into an unheated cast iron pot.

- The sky is hazy or partly cloudy.

- Cooking is done in the morning or late afternoon.

- You are within three months of the Winter Solstice.

- The cooker is rarely repositioned.

- The food consists of a single large mass, such as a whole winter squash.

- You are cooking a large volume of food, such as a large stew.

CHAPTER FOUR
Pots & pans for solar cooking

Solar cooking requires the use of dark-colored pots and pans. As explained in Chapter One, dark colors absorb sunlight, while light colors reflect light away. Different types of pots and pans have different characteristics that affect preheating time, cooking time, and other factors.

Use dark colored pots and pans

- While black is the best heat absorption color, other dark colors like seasoned cast iron, brown or dark blue Pyrex and gray non-stick bakeware are dark enough. In fact, all you really need is a dark lid. Mix and match pots and lids as needed.

- The most popular solar cooking pot is a round, covered, 3-liter (10" diameter) black, speckled graniteware roaster available at many supermarkets, camping stores, and online retailers such as Solar Cookers International.

- The lid of a 3-liter graniteware roaster fits perfectly on a 9" pie plate or cast iron skillet.

- A matte finish absorbs heat better than a shiny finish. However, the ubiquitous graniteware roaster is shiny, and works great.

- Another option is to paint your favorite stainless steel or aluminum pots black on the outside with non-toxic barbecue or poster paint.

- Make a small cheap cooking pot by painting a canning jar black. Leave an unpainted stripe down the side so you can watch the food cooking. One advantage to a canning jar is that it acts as a pressure cooker. When a sealed canning jar is heated, the pressure builds up inside. Canning jars are made from tempered glass designed to withstand heat and steam build-up. Two-piece metal canning jar lids keep the jar sealed yet release dangerous levels of steam when necessary. Never try to use an ordinary glass jar this way — they are not made with tempered glass and their lids cannot release excess steam.

- A few dark foods can be cooked without a lid, such as black beans, chocolate baked goods. Cookies, crackers, granola and a few other foods are baked uncovered on baking sheets to make them crispy.

- Avoid low-fired earthenware pots, such as red clay roasters. They act more like insulators than heat conductors.

My solar cookware collection

- Two 3-liter black speckled graniteware roasters. These are my "everyday" pots. I also use both the bottoms and the tops as lids for other pots and pans.

- A smaller black graniteware roaster I found at an antique store that fits perfectly around a 1-quart bundt cake mold.

- A shiny stainless steel 5-quart pot that barely fits in my solar cooker. I use the pot with a black lid from another pot.

- Three Pyrex pans: a dark blue pie plate, a brown 1-quart covered casserole dish, a brown bread pan.

- A dark gray oven roasting pan rescued from the dumpster that I use as a cookie sheet and for toasting foods.

- A black metal nonstick 9" x 13" covered casserole pan. I use the bottom as a cover for the cookie sheet.

- Three cast iron pans: a 6-inch enameled skillet, a corn bread pan divided into eight wedges, and a 9" tortilla griddle.

- A gray non-stick bread pan and a very large bread pan that has been spray-painted black.

Solar cookware entrepreneur needed!

Someday, I hope, solar cooking will become so popular that someone will manufacture a special line of black, covered pots and pans designed to work with common solar cooker designs. Unfortunately, finding an appropriately-sized, dark-colored pot or pan is sometimes difficult. For example, large graniteware roasters do not fit into many commercial solar cooker models such as the Sun Oven™. I spent weeks searching for a black 9" x 13" covered baking dish suitable for making lasagna. I finally found one made by Kaiser Bakeware, only to discover when it arrived that one of the handles was ½-inch too long to fit inside my Sun Oven™. My husband had to crudely saw off the handle for me, but it works great anyway.

If you decide to build your own cooker, design the interior to be large enough to accommodate your favorite pots year-round (the Sun Oven™, which has tilted glazing and an adjustable back rod, loses some of its interior volume when the glazing is tilted back to capture the high summer sun).

Pot shapes and sizes

- Thin-walled lightweight pots like enameled graniteware heat up and cool down quickly. Glass and cast-iron pots and pans heat up more slowly but retain their heat longer. On partly cloudy days, thick-walled pots retain their heat during short periods of intermittent clouds.
- Flatter pots and pans heat up faster than pots with higher sides.
- For optimum heating efficiency, fill a cooking pot roughly half-full with food or liquid. The air above the food helps to retain cooking heat and provides added insulation. Lack of air space in a pot results in lower temperatures. Too much air space dissipates cooking heat too fast.

Regulating the moisture level

Solar cookers are naturally moist. However, it possible to regulate moisture retention or evaporation inside a solar cooker or cooking pot.

- To keep the moisture sealed in the cooking pot, a tight lid is necessary. Otherwise, moisture will seep out of the pot and condense inside the glazing or cooking bag, impeding the entry of light into the cooker and lowering the temperature. When using a graniteware roaster, office-style binder clips can be used to seal the lid tightly to the pot.

- If no lid is available, a black cloth can be draped over the pot. The cloth will absorb moisture released by the food.
- If you live in an arid climate, you can vent the lid and cooker by propping the lid slightly askew and leaving a small (1/16" or smaller) gap in the cooker seal to allow excess steam to escape. In my Sun Oven™, I prevent moisture buildup inside the oven by not sealing the glazing latch. The downside is this will slightly lower the cooker efficiency because some heat will escape along with the moisture. Where I live, this is not a problem.
- Crispy cookies, nuts, granola and a few other foods are cooked on an uncovered tray to allow moisture to escape.
- If there is a lot of moisture buildup inside the cooker, it will condense and trickle down to the bottom. If necessary, wipe up moisture with a sponge and allow the cooker to dry out before storing.

Positioning pots in a solar cooker

- In some box cookers such as the Sun Oven™, pots are raised above the bottom of the cooker so that hot air can circulate underneath the pot.
- The closer the food is to the top of the oven and glazing, the hotter it will get. Ways to raise a pot include blocks of wood, canning rings and metal trivets. Barbara Kerr likes to use three small, black oiled stones. Some commercial ovens come with an internal shelf.
- In box cookers with a large, flat metal floor, pots are placed directly on the floor. The floor transfers much of the heat through conduction into the pot. Pots can also be placed directly on the floor of panel cookers.
- If you have a large box cooker, place larger pots and harder-to-cook foods at the back of the cooker where it will receive the most direct sunlight.

Downward view of a large box cooker

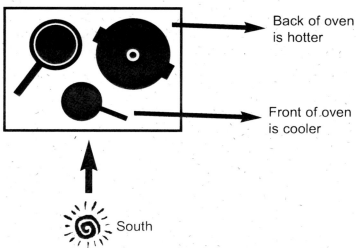

Back of oven is hotter

Front of oven is cooler

South

CHAPTER FIVE
Solar cooking methods

It is possible to use a solar cooker for everything from simmering to blanching, poaching, steaming, sautéing, braising, baking, roasting, toasting, grilling and pan frying. Most of these methods can be done in a box cooker. A few require the extra high temperatures only achievable with a parabolic reflector. Use the following tips to adapt your favorite recipes to solar cooking.

Boiling and simmering

Boiling and simmering is the process of cooking food submersed in water or another liquid that is at the boiling point. No matter what the temperature of a solar cooker or stove may be, the temperature of a boiling liquid will never rise above the boiling point (When molecules of water reach the boiling point, they evaporate). The boiling point is only 212°F/100°C at sea level, and lower at high altitudes (199°F/93°C at 7,000 feet in Flagstaff, Arizona). Most foods, including beans, grains, oatmeal, soup, sauce, polenta, fruit preserves and vegetable stock only require a slow simmer.

To simmer foods in a solar box cooker, place the food and cooking liquid in an appropriately-sized pot (filled ideally about half-way full for the most efficient heating). Use a little less liquid than you would use if simmering on a stovetop. A 3-liter graniteware roaster is best for most foods. Cover pot and place in cooker. Because water is a "thermal mass" that requires significant energy inputs in order to rise in temperature, the heating up time is longer than on a stovetop burner, which has a very high energy output. A small pot of grains might take 15 to 30 minutes to heat up to the boiling point in a box cooker, while a large pot of stew might take two hours to begin to boil. However, once the food or liquid is heated to the boiling point, the simmering time is exactly the same as on a stovetop.

A parabolic reflector heats up food as fast as a stovetop burner.

Slow cooking

Electric slow cookers (crock pots) have recently made a comeback. Recipes designed for slow cookers are easily adapted to box and panel cookers. Like solar cookers, slow cookers cook at low to moderate temperatures and are moist. Slow cookers have three temperature settings: Low (200°F/93°C), Medium (250°F/ 121°C) and High (300°F/ 149°C). To adapt a slow cooker recipe to a solar cooker, simply adjust the cooking time to take into account the temperature difference, if any. Food cooked at 300°F/149°C cooks in approximately half the time of food cooked at 200°F/93°C. If the food is placed in the solar cooker in the morning and the cooker is pointed due south for absentee cooking, the cooking time is similar to a slow cooker set on Low for approximately eight hours.

Blanching/parboiling

Blanching or parboiling is the partial cooking of a food by plunging it into boiling water for a few seconds or minutes and then transferring the food to ice-cold water to stop the cooking process. For example, tomatoes and peppers are blanched to allow the skins to be easily slipped off. Vegetables and fruit are often blanched before drying or freezing to preserve their color and nutrients. Some vegetables, including green beans, Brussels sprouts and kale, are blanched to tenderize them before stir-frying. Blanching can also be done in a solar cooker without a pot of boiling water. Instead, vegetables can be steamed or sweated for a short time, until the skin is cooked, but the insides are still raw.

Steeping or poaching below the boiling point

Many foods, including grains, beans, tea, poached eggs and fruit, begin to cook before the boiling point is reached. Therefore, these foods need only be steeped in hot water, not actually simmered. Poaching technically begins at around 160°F/71°C. Even on a partly cloudy day, steeping and poaching is easy in a solar cooker.

Steaming

Steamed food is cooked by suspending it over boiling water in a tightly covered pot. The trapped steam increases the air pressure inside the pot, which actually raises the boiling point above 212°F/100°C and thus can cook food faster than simmering (the boiling point rises with increased air pressure). Vegetables, filled dumplings and steamed breads and cakes are commonly steamed foods. Solar steaming is very similar to stovetop steaming. The easiest way to do it is to place a collapsing steamer basket or metal trivet inside a 3-liter graniteware roaster. Fill the roaster with an inch or so of water, but not enough to rise above the bottom of the steamer basket. Preheat the pot and water in your solar cooker until you see steam begin to condense on the cooker's glazing or the inside of the oven cooking bag. Place the food in the steamer and steam for approximately the same amount of time as for stovetop steaming. Steamed breads and cakes take 50 percent longer in a solar cooker.

Sweating

Sweating is similar to steaming, except that the food is cooked directly in a covered pot in its own juices or with a very small amount of added liquid. Sweating is the easiest way to cook in a solar cooker.

Sauteing

Sautéing involves cooking food quickly in a small amount of fat at a temperature above the boiling point, usually at least 300°F/149°C. Sautéing seals in flavor and lightly browns food. Small amounts of food can be sautéed in a solar cooker, including onions, garlic, chiles, ginger, whole spices and small diced veggies. If possible, preheat a cast iron skillet. Otherwise, use a pie plate or 3-liter graniteware roaster. Add the oil and heat it before adding the food, just like on a stovetop. Never try to sauté more than a single layer of food. Keep the pan uncovered. Once the fat is sizzling, food sautés in exactly the same amount of time as on a stovetop. Don't let it burn!

Braising

To braise foods, chop them into small pieces, briefly sauté them uncovered, then cover and allow the food to sweat in its own juices.

Baking, roasting and toasting

Baking, roasting and toasting involve cooking foods using dry heat. This may seem like an oxymoron since solar cookers are moister than conventional ovens. However, foods can be cooked without water in a solar cooker, and will even lightly brown. In fact, foods left too long in a multiple reflector oven will burn if left unattended too long. Foods that are baked, roasted or toasted include baked goods, browned cubes of tofu and tempeh, toasted nuts and seeds, and granola. Baked goods are baked in covered graniteware roasters, cast iron skillets, flat casserole dishes, pie plates and muffin pans. Cookies, granola and nuts are baked on an uncovered baking sheet. Depending on your style of cooker, the cooking time ranges from just a little longer than a conventional oven to several hours longer.

Grilling, broiling and frying

A parabolic reflector is necessary to achieve the high temperatures needed for these cooking methods. Grilling and broiling involve cooking food using intense direct heat. Food quickly browns on the outside, producing a characteristic grilled flavor. Foods to be grilled are sliced thin enough for their insides to cook thoroughly in the time it takes to brown the outside. Foods are usually marinated or basted with oil just prior to grilling. Use an oiled grill pan just like on a stovetop. Parabolic reflectors are also great for frying pancakes, French toast, deep frying fritters or French fries, etc.

Solar cooking times

Fast cooking foods

Grains, oatmeal, polenta, small lentils, fruit, "above ground" vegetables (such as artichokes, corn, eggplant, green beans, leafy greens, peppers, tomatoes), small diced root vegetables, tofu, tempeh, seitan, reheated leftovers, nachos, eggs and dairy.

Moderate cooking foods

Presoaked dried beans, large lentils, split peas, whole root vegetables, casseroles containing precooked foods (such as lasagna and enchiladas), small loaves of bread, open face pies, cookies.

Slow cooking foods

Unsoaked dried beans, large loaves of bread, double crust pies, large whole winter squash, large pots of water, broth or stew, casseroles containing uncooked grains and pasta, whole tofu roasts.

PART II

Solar recipes

The most important thing to remember
You do NOT need special recipes to cook in a solar cooker. ANY recipe can be adjusted for solar cooking.

The following recipes were tested in a preheated Sun Oven™ with four reflectors at 7,000 feet altitude in the sunny Southwest. The boiling point at this altitude is only 199°F/93°C, but the sunshine is very strong. My Sun Oven™ hovers between 300–325°F/149–163°C on sunny days and 200–250°F/93–121°C on partly cloudy days. If you have a cooker that reaches lower temperatures or if the sky is hazy or partly cloudy, most dishes will still cook fine. In most cases, they'll just take a little longer to cook than the times stated here.

CHAPTER SIX
Preheating, defrosting & melting

Basic method: Place food or liquid in a covered pot. Aim the cooker toward the sun and cook until food is heated through. Preheating and melting don't require much time and can be done in partly cloudy conditions. Heating a pot of water to the boiling point requires full sunlight.

❋ Preheating your cooker ❋

Preheating a solar box oven greatly speeds up the actual cooking time. If you open the cooker early in the morning, esepcially during the colder months, the cooker may take up to an hour or more to reach maximum temperature. During the middle of the day, preheating may take only 30 minutes. In some climates, you must be careful not to leave multiple reflector ovens empty for too long, or they will rise above 450°F/232°C, causing the paint on the inside of the cooker to start smoking off. To moderate the temperature while preheating, place a cast iron pot, rock or brick inside the cooker to absorb some of the heat. Panel cookers can also be preheated if you are cooking inside an ovetrurned glass bowl.

❋ Preheating cast iron pots and pans ❦

Preheating cast iron cookware considerably speeds up food cooking time. Add 15–30 minutes to the oven preheating time.

❋ Heating water in a solar cooker ❦

Preheat a pot of water in a covered pot for making coffee, tea, soup stock, blanching vegetables, water bath canning, water pasteurization, etc. Do you really need instructions on heating water in a solar cooker? Yes! It is important to keep in mind that water is a dense material known as a "thermal mass." Liquids require a lot of heat to warm up just a few degrees. Parabolic reflectors heat water as quickly as do stovetop burners. Box cookers heat water faster than panel cookers. In a box cooker, a single cup of water may take 30–40 minutes to be brought to boiling. Boiling several quarts of water can take four or more hours. Clear, sunny conditions are needed to boil water in a reasonable period of time. For the greatest efficiency, fill a pot about halfway with liquid.

❋ Heating refrigerated leftovers ❦

A single meal takes only about 20 minutes to heat up in a preheated box cooker. Covered 1-quart casserole dishes and canning jars that have been painted black work well for heating small volumes of food. Take a solar cooker to work and make it available for preparing lunch, coffee, tea and snacks!

❋ Melting stuff ❋

Solar cookers are great for melting all sorts of things, such as coconut oil, Earth Balance™, butter, chocolate, sugar, crystallized honey, jam (for glazing cakes and pie crusts), and wax. If you have a low-temperature solar cooker such as a panel cooker or reflectorless box cooker, place the food in a covered pot and leave it in the cooker until it melts. Higher-temperature cookers are similar to a microwave or stovetop burner. If using a multiple reflector box cooker, either use the above method and make sure the ingredients are not left in the cooker long enough to burn, or preheat water in a double boiler before adding the stuff to melt.
If using a parabolic cooker, use a double boiler the same way you would on a stovetop.

❋ Nachos ❋

Spread tortilla chips across a dark baking sheet or casserole dish. Spoon on beans and other toppings. Sprinkle cheese on top and bake uncovered until the cheese melts.

❋ Defrosting frozen foods ❋

To defrost frozen food, simply place the food in a covered pot and leave it in the cooker until it is no longer frozen. An individual frozen meal will defrost in about an hour.

❊ Frozen foods & absentee cooking ❊

This method is great for items such as a tofu roast or large volume of frozen stew. For all-day absentee cooking, place a large portion of frozen food in a covered pot into a box or panel cooker in the morning. Orient the cooker due south. You do not need to worry about microbe contamination unless clouds obscure the sun for a significant period of time — enough to cause the temperature of the cooker to drop below 140°F/60°C for more than two hours. See food safety information in Chapter Three: Solar cooking basics.

Using the absentee cooking method to defrost and cook frozen foods

In the morning, orient the cooker due south. During the morning, the food will slowly heat up. During midday, the food will cook. In the afternoon, the food will slowly cool down and be ready for dinner. If necessary, you can keep the food food warm for a couple of hours after sunset by throwing a blanket or some pillows on top of a box cooker (with the reflectors(s) folded down over the cooker if there are any). See Chapter Twenty: Fireless cooking for more information on insulating food to keep it warm.

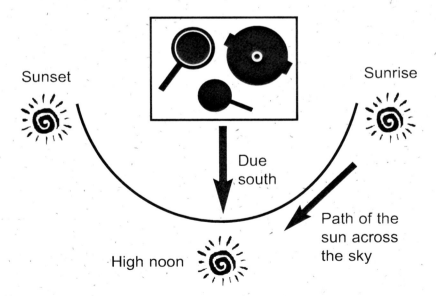

Sunset

Sunrise

Due south

High noon

Path of the sun across the sky

CHAPTER SEVEN

Grains, polenta & porridge

Basic method: Mix the grains and cooking liquid in a pot, cover, and cook until done. Occasionally, some stirring may be necessary. Because grains don't need to reach the boiling point to cook, partly cloudy conditions and low temperature box and panel cookers work as well as higher temperature cookers.

❋ Basic grain cooking ❋

Grains can be cooked in plain water, vegetable broth, milk, wine, beer or a combination of liquids. Highly acidic liquids like tomato or apple juice slow down the cooking time considerably and are not recommended. Add a little salt, tamari or miso if desired. Large volumes of grain will take longer to heat up to the boiling point than smaller volumes. Directions for optional pre-toasting of grains for a nuttier flavor can be found in Chapter Seventeen: Toasting nuts, seeds, granola & more.

The usual ratio of grains to liquid is 1:2. However, grains cooked in a solar box or panel cooker need less cooking liquid, due to the slower rate of evaporation.

The following simmering times are based on 1 ½ cups dry grain + 2 ¾ cups liquid in a preheated cooker:
⚘ Fine bulgur: preheat boiling water and stir into grain
⚘ Amaranth, coarse bulgur, buckwheat, tef: 20–30 minutes
⚘ Quinoa, buckwheat and sushi rice: 1 hour
⚘ Brown rice and millet: 1 ½ hours.
⚘ Whole wheat, rye berries, barley, oat groats: 2 hours
⚘ Add another 20–30 minutes to the cooking time if you are cooking grains in a thick liquid such as coconut milk

⚘ Quinoa tabbouli ⚘

Tabbouli is a marinated grain salad traditionally made with bulgur. Millet and rice are also excellent in this recipe. Add ½–1 cup cooked beans, fresh peas or shelled edamame for a more substantial dish. **3–4 servings**

1 cup rinsed quinoa
1 ¾ cups water
Pinch salt
½ cup fresh or 3 tablespoons dried spearmint
½ cup fresh or ¼ cup dried flat or curly-leaved parsley
1/3 cup diced green onions or chives
1 cup chopped tomatoes, strawberries or tangerine sections
¼ cup olive or canola oil
2 tablespoons one of the following: lemon or lime juice, or rice/cider/white wine vinegar
Salt to taste

1. Combine quinoa, water and salt, cover and cook until done.
2. Pour cooked quinoa into a large mixing bowl to cool for 15–30 minutes.
3. Add rest of ingredients and toss gently to mix. Chill at least 30 minutes before serving to allow flavors to combine.

❋ Grain pilafs ❋

It's easy to make pilafs in a solar cooker. For quick-cooking grains, add diced vegetables, dried fruit, dried herbs and spices at the beginning of cooking. For longer cooking grains, add other ingredients about halfway through. Mix in chopped nuts and seeds, sweeteners and fresh herbs after cooking.

❋ Risotto and sweet grain puddings ❋

Risotto is a creamy rice dish traditionally made from Italian Arborio rice. It normally requires constant stirring on the stovetop to prevent burning. In a solar box or panel cooker, you can make risotto and creamy grain puddings with no stirring! Grains that work especially well for this purpose include rice, bulgur, millet, whole oats, dry-toasted steel cut oats, barley and quinoa. Use a little bit more liquid than usual and cook for 20 percent longer than usual. The cooking liquid can be vegetable broth, milk, coconut milk, creamed corn or cooked vegetables puréed with broth (like pumpkin or tomatoes). Savory risottos are traditionally flavored with a sauté of onions, leeks, shallots or garlic and seasonal herbs. The dry grain is stirred into the sauté before the cooking liquid is added (see Chapter Ten: Sautés, roux & gravy).

❋ Posole ❋

Posole, also known as hominy, is whole dent or flint corn that has been soaked in slaked lime (calcium hydroxide, $Ca(OH)_2$). Liming increases the niacin (vitamin B3) availability in the corn. Fresh and frozen posole is available at supermarkets in the Southwest. If you live outside the Southwest, order dried posole online. Native Seeds/SEARCH, a nonprofit heirloom seed bank in Tucson, Arizona, sells organic blue corn posole (www.nativeseeds.org).

If using dried posole, presoak the kernels in water for at least 8 hours, just as you would soak dried beans. I like to simmer hydrated posole in vegetable stock with an added vegetable bouillon cube. If I don't have homemade stock available, I use Imagine Food's No Chicken Broth. Posole takes about 4 hours to simmer in a solar box oven. When posole is cooked, it blossoms like underwater popcorn. Posole is delicious when added to spicy stews and chilies. It has a bland corny flavor and soaks up the flavors of other ingredients. If desired, simmer soaked posole with unsoaked dried beans; they cook in about the same amount of time. Posole can also be eaten as a side dish, marinated in grain salads or added to gratin casseroles.

❋ Rolled and cracked grain porridges ❦

In addition to oatmeal, many other grains can be rolled, flaked or coarsely ground to make porridge. For example, quinoa is available flaked. Cracked grains like steel cut oats take longer to cook than rolled grains. Furthermore, whole amaranth and tef make excellent porridges because they have a naturally mucilaginous texture just like oatmeal due to high amounts of soluble fiber. Porridges range from thin to thick depending on the preferences of the cook. Try a 1:2 ratio of grain to liquid and adjust as desired. Traditional Irish and Scottish cooks add oatmeal to boiling water for a less mushy texture. To follow this method, preheat the water in your cooker until boiling and then stir in the rolled grains. Otherwise, just mix the unheated water and grain together. Cover and cook until done. A single bowl of regular rolled oats takes about 15 minutes in a preheated cooker on a sunny day.

❋ Popcorn ❦

Making popcorn requires a parabolic reflector. Just like making popcorn on a stovetop, use a covered heavy-bottomed pot, a little oil and a single layer of popcorn kernels. Because the lid must be cracked a little to let out excess steam, a few kernels might jump out of the pot.

Polenta

Unlike its traditional cousin, solar polenta requires no stirring! Polenta is a northern Italian word that refers to both the porridge and a dish created when the porridge is spread out to cool. Other names for polenta include mush, grits and mamaliga (Romanian). Before corn arrived in Europe from the New World, people made polenta from many different grains and legumes, including acorns, barley, buckwheat, fava beans, garbanzo beans, millet, rye and wheat (farina). For example, polenta nera, *"black polenta" made from buckwheat grits, is a favorite dish in northern Italy.*

Polenta has the best texture when made with medium to coarse meal, although flour works too. For grain polentas, use a ratio of 1 part meal to 3–4 parts liquid. Bean polentas work best with a ratio of 1 ½ parts legume flour to 2 ½–3 parts liquid. Simmering liquids can include water, broth and milk. Add salt, fresh or dried herbs, dried tomatoes, sweeteners, olive oil or other fats, and other ingredients to the mixture as desired. Whisk together the grits and liquid in the cooking pot, cover, and cook about an hour. Whisk once halfway through to ensure even cooking (the top will dry out otherwise).

Polenta can be eaten warm, or spread out to cool on a greased baking sheet or wooden board. It will start to solidify immediately. Cool for at least 30 minutes, or refrigerate for up to two days. Eat it sliced, fried, baked or grilled for a variety of different textures and flavors. Serve any time of day with either sweet and savory toppings, including syrups, sauces, gravies, and sautéed or grilled vegetables. Polenta can also be used as a pizza or pie crust, spread on top of a pot pie or sliced and used in place of lasagna noodles in casserole dishes.

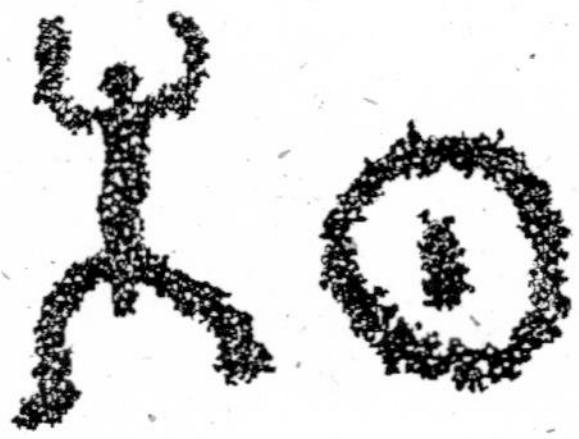

❉ Baked polenta ❦

Slice cooled polenta into ¼–½ inch thick slabs. Preheat
cooker. Arrange slices on a dark, greased baking sheet. Use a
pastry brush to baste polenta with olive oil. Cover sheet with a
dark lid (or another baking sheet), preferably one that will
allow air circulation around the edges to facilitate evaporation
of excess moisture. I use an overturned 9" x 13" black metal
casserole dish as a lid beacuse it is slightly narrower than my
baking sheet. Bake 1–2 ½ hours. A shorter cooking time produces a creamy texture; bake longer for a crispy, lightly
browned crust.

❉ Garbanzo "French fries" ❦

*This remarkable low-fat recipe tastes a bit like French fries. I
grind my own coarse garbanzo flour in a hand grinder for a
toothy texture. Coarse garbanzo flour is also available in
Indian grocery stores. Fine flour produces a flaky, biscuit-like
texture. Serve with ketchup, just like the real thing.* **2–6 servings**

¾ cup garbanzo flour
1 ½ cups vegetable broth
(I prefer Imagine Food's No Chicken Broth)
1 bouillon cube or pinch of salt

1. In cooking pot, whisk ingredients.
Cover. Simmer 45 minutes–1 hour or
until thick. Whisk once halfway
through cooking.
2. Pour into a ¼–1/3-inch thick
slab and cool.
3. Slice into "French fries" ¼–1
inch wide x 2–4 inches long. Arrange
in a greased casserole dish without
touching. Lightly baste the tops with oil.
Cover and bake in a preheated cooker until
lightly browned and crispy.

CHAPTER EIGHT
Beans, lentils & split peas

Basic method: Solar cooking beans, lentils and split peas is by far my favorite way to cook legumes. As long as the beans are kept submerged under water or vegetable broth the entire cooking time, they will not burn and need almost no attention at all, except to occasionally re-aim the cooker toward the sun.

❋ Solar beans ❋

I usually cook legumes ahead of time when I have available cooker space and refrigerate or freeze them for later use. Old beans can take more than twice as long to cook as beans from this year's crop. **2–4 servings**

1 cup of dried beans, lentils or split peas
Minimum of 2 ½ cups liquid (add more as needed to cover)

Beans
- Presoaked: 3–4 hours
- Unsoaked: 5–6 hours
- Presoaked runner beans: 6–8 hours

Lentils, split peas and channa dal (split baby garbanzo beans)
- Tiny red lentils: 20 minutes
- Large brown lentils and channa dal: 2 hours
- Dissolved lentils and split peas for making soup: 3–4 hours
- Presoak lentils and split peas for faster cooking and an especially creamy texture.

Two bean cooking myths debunked

It is not necessary to drain the soaking water
Contrary to the popular myth that soaking removes the sugars in legumes that cause digestive problems for many people, these sugars are not water-soluble. Russ Parsons writes in his excellent kitchen chemistry book How to Read a French Fry that, "(T)hese sugars are the seed's stores of energy for germination and growth. Since soaking is also the first step in germinating, it wouldn't make sense for the seed to give up these all-important sugars so easily." Cooking beans in their soaking water saves water, vitamins and minerals.

It is OK to add salt to beans while they are cooking
Most cookbooks state never to add salt to cooking beans, in the erroneous belief that salt toughens the skins and prevents the beans from softening. However, this is not true. For example, kombu, a salty seaweed, is added to bean-pots in Japanese macrobiotic cooking. Even at 7,000 feet altitude, I have noticed no difference in cooking time between salted and unsalted beans. I like to add a bouillon cube to a pot of beans for extra flavor.

❉ Flavorful bean pots, dals and soups ❦

Make flavorful legume dishes by adding herbs and spices to cooking beans. A few suggestions: vegetable broth, halved or quartered onions (leave on root end), whole garlic cloves, dried chiles, whole spices like cumin and caraway seeds, epazote (a leafy Mexican herb in the mint family traditionally added to beans), and a little salt. Never add acidic ingredients (tomato juice, ketchup) or high-mineral ingredients (molasses) to cooking beans; the beans will not soften.

❉ Refried beans/hummus ❦

To make bean dips, cook beans with diced onion and garlic and mash after cooking, or cook beans separately, then sauté onions and garlic in oil and mash with the beans (Chapter Ten: Sautés, roux & gravy). I add ½ cup TVP chili mix, available in the bulk section of natural foods stores, and a little water to beans during the last 15–30 minutes of cooking.

❉ Baked beans ❦

Fully precook beans before making baked beans in a solar cooker. Other good flavorings include ketchup, mustard, apple butter and barbeque sauce. **2–4 servings**

2 cups cooked beans (white, black, pinto, garbanzo, etc.)
¼ cup maple/agave/rice syrup, molasses or honey
3 tablespoons tomato paste
1 cup vegetable broth or bean cooking liquid
1 tablespoon dried minced onion or 2 tablespoons fresh
Garlic salt to taste

1. Mix ingredients in a 1-quart casserole dish. The beans should have a soupy consistency.
2. Cover and bake 2 hours for a syrupy texture, or up to 3 hours for a crusty top.

❋ Cuban black beans ❋

This recipe is sized for a 3-liter graniteware roaster. Serve over rice, quinoa or orzo pasta. Make black bean soup by blending some of the cooked beans with some broth and returning them to the pot, adding broth as necessary to achieve desired consistency. **6–8 servings**

1-¼–1 ½ cups dry black turtle beans
(or 2 ½–3 ½ cups precooked)
Water for presoaking (optional)
Vegetable broth as needed for cooking
2 onions, quartered
¼ teaspoon salt or bouillon cube
1 large dried chile (optional)
1 bay leaf
1–4 minced garlic cloves
1 tablespoon olive or canola oil
1 green bell pepper, diced
1 red, yellow or orange bell pepper, diced
1 teaspoon ground cumin, toasted or untoasted
1 teaspoon ground coriander, toasted or untoasted
1–2 teaspoons dried flaked oregano
or 1–2 tablespoons fresh leaves, minced
Salt to taste
Ketchup, vinegar, lemon or lime juice to taste
Garnish with sour cream or yogurt (optional)

1. Presoak beans if desired. Cook the beans with broth, onion, chile, bay leaf and bouillon or salt until soft. Remove onion and chile and discard. Drain beans and set aside.
2. Dice second onion and sauté with garlic in the oil in pot until onions are clear. (Chapter Ten: Sautés, roux & gravy). Add bell peppers and spices and cook until peppers are soft, about 1 hour. Add beans and heat through, 30 minutes–1 hour.
3. Season with salt and ketchup or a dash of vinegar, lemon or lime juice. Serve with yogurt, sour cream, or more ketchup.

❋ Golden split pea soup ❋

*This recipe is sized for a 3-liter graniteware roaster. Use any
lentil or split pea variety as desired. Yellow split peas create a
beautiful golden-color. Enhance the color theme with yellow
potatoes, yellow carrots, yellow tomatoes and turmeric.
Chipotle peppers add a smoked flavor to the soup, a spicy
vegetarian alternative to smoked ham or bacon. Another good
addition is to add a handful of tender leafy greens near the
end of cooking. I make up a huge pot of this soup and freeze it
in individual servings for days when I don't feel like cooking.*
6–8 servings

1 ¼–1 ½ cups split peas, lentils or channa dal
(or 2 ½–3 ½ cups precooked)
Vegetable stock as needed
2 onions
1–2 bouillon cubes or ½ teaspoon salt
1–2 dried chipotle chiles (optional)
1–3 tablespoons olive or canola oil
1–3 minced garlic cloves, minced
2–3 medium carrots, diced
2 medium Yukon Gold or other potatoes, diced (unpeeled)
2 stalks celery or 2 teaspoons dried lovage
1 14-oz can diced stewed tomatoes
or 2 cups skinned tomatoes, diced (optional)
1 teaspoon whole fennel seeds or ground fennel
1 teaspoon whole coriander seeds or ground coriander
¼ teaspoon turmeric (optional)
1 teaspoon while nigella seeds or ground nigella (optional)
Dash cayenne, black pepper or curry powder (optional)
½ cup fresh chopped cilantro or green onions (optional)
Garnish with bacon bits or fried onions (optional)

1. Presoak split peas if desired. Simmer beans in broth, with
one quartered onion, the chipotle chiles and bouillon or salt
until split peas begin to dissolve into the broth.
2. Dice second onion and sauté with garlic in the oil until
onions are clear. (See Chapter Ten: Sautés, roux & gravy).

3. Add potatoes, carrots, celery, whole spices and ½ cup broth. Cover and cook until potatoes are soft, 30 minutes–1 hour.

4. Add split peas, tomatoes, ground spices and 1–2 cups broth as desired to pot. Cook another 30 minutes–1 hour (or longer if lentils/split peas were taken directly out of the refrigerator) until heated through.

5. Remove pot from cooker and stir in fresh cilantro or green onions. Serve with bacon bits or fried onions.

❧ Marinated garbanzo bean salad ❦

Beans and whole lentils make an excellent salad when marinated in oil and vinegar, lemon or lime juice. **4–8 servings**

4 cups cooked garbanzo beans
¼ cup olive oil
1–3 minced garlic cloves
2 tablespoons white wine or rice vinegar
2 teaspoons prepared mustard (optional)
½ cup chopped cilantro, basil or parsley
¼ cup sliced green onions
½ cup sliced olives (your favorite kind)
½ teaspoon cracked red pepper (optional)
Salt to taste

1. Drain cooked beans and place in mixing bowl.
2. Sauté garlic in oil in small saucepan (Chapter Ten: Sautés, roux & gravy). Remove from cooker and cool 10 minutes. Pour sauté into small bowl and whisk in vinegar and mustard.
3. Pour marinade over beans. Stir in herbs, onions, olives and pepper. Salt to taste. Toss well.
4. Chill several hours before serving to combine flavors. Serve cold or at room temperature.

CHAPTER NINE
Pasta & dumplings

Basic method: Pasta is simmered in a solar box or panel cooker using equal volumes of pasta and water. The pasta absorbs nearly all the liquid as it cooks. Use a covered, tinted glass casserole dish to watch the water being absorbed and make it easier to remove the pot before the pasta overcooks.

❊ Plain pasta ❊

Short shapes such as macaroni, rotelli or orzo work better than spagetti or fettucine. **2–4 servings**

2 cups water or vegetable broth
2 cups dried pasta
1 tablespoon olive or canola oil
1 teaspoon salt (optional)

1. Preheat water or broth in 1-quart casserole dish.
2. When you see steam begin to collect on the underside of the glazing or oven cooking bag, toss pasta with oil, and add to boiling water. Cover and cook until done, roughly the same amount of time as stovetop boiling (9–12 minutes at sea level).

✳ Macaroni and cheese ✳

For centuries, Italians have boiled dry pasta in almond milk. As the pasta cooks, a white sauce forms, thickened by the starch in the pasta. Pasta takes at least 50 percent longer to cook in milk than in water. The recipe can be made plain or seasoned with herbs and spices like oregano or dried tomatoes.

4 servings

3 ½ cups almond milk or other nondairy milk
¼ cup cornstarch, potato starch or arrowroot powder
1–3 tablespoons olive or canola oil
1–3 minced garlic cloves
or ¼ teaspoon garlic powder (optional)
1 medium chopped onion
or 1 teaspoon onion powder (optional)
Salt to taste or 1 bouillon cube
2 cups dry pasta
1–2 tablespoons raw nut butter
or up to 1/3 cup grated cheese (optional)
¼ cup untoasted bread crumbs (optional)

1. Preheat 3 ¼ cups of the milk and salt or bouillon in the cooker until the liquid begins to steam.
2. Coat pasta with oil and set aside momentarily.
3. Mix ¼ cup milk and the starch. Remove simmering pot from cooker. Quickly whisk in the starch mixture. The sauce will immediately begin to thicken.
4. Stir in pasta, nut butter or cheese, herbs and spices.
5. Cover and cook 30–45 minutes, or until pasta has softened and absorbed about half the sauce.
6. Remove pot from cooker. Sprinkle bread crumbs on top if desired and serve or place back in the cooker (uncovered) for about 15 minutes to lightly brown bread crumbs.

✹ Sweet noodle kugel ✹

Kugel is the German word for pudding. Follow the macaroni and cheese recipe on previous page. Leave out the cheese, bouillon and savory herbs. Flavor dish with sweeteners, fruit, nuts and sweet spices like cinnamon. Breadcrumbs, cookie crumbs or ground nuts are excellent as a crunchy topping.

✹ Large soup dumplings ✹

For soup dumplings 1 ½ inches or larger in diameter, such as matzo balls, bring a pot of water or broth to a boil. Cover and simmer dumplings 30 minutes, or until tender but not mushy.

✹ Stuffed pastas ✹

Everything from Tibetan momos to spring rolls, pot stickers and pierogi can be cooked in a solar cooker. Steaming produces a soft-textured dumpling while baking creates a crispy, lightly browned crust.

Steaming

1. Fill a cooking pot with 1 inch of water. Lightly oil an expandable steamer tray and insert into pot. Cover and heat until water is boiling.
2. Place the dumplings on steamer rack spaced at least ½ inch apart.
3. Steam 15–30 minutes, depending on dumplings' size or until dough is al dente.

Baking

1. Arrange dumplings on a greased baking sheet. To prevent the surface of the dumplings from drying out as they bake, use a pastry brush to lightly oil the exposed dough.
2. Cover sheet or pan with a dark lid, preferably one that allows some air circulation, and bake 20–30 minutes, or until dough is lightly browned.

❉ Couscous ❦

Couscous is a tiny, grain-like North African pasta made from semolina or other grains such as millet. Solar couscous is exceptionally fluffy. For a sweet breakfast or dessert pudding, cook couscous in milk and season with sweeteners, dessert spices and dried fruit. 3–6 servings

1 tablespoon olive oil, canola oil
or melted Earth Balance™ or coconut oil
1 cup couscous
Several sprigs fresh herbs (optional)
1 ¾ cups vegetable broth or water
1 vegetable bouillon cube or salt to taste

1. Sauté couscous in the oil by thoroughly mixing the two ingredients, covering and baking about 20 minutes, or until couscous begins to brown. Do not let burn!
2. Add broth, salt and herbs. Be careful; the liquid will sputter when it meets the hot couscous. Cover. Cook about 30 minutes, until liquid is absorbed and couscous is light and fluffy.
3. Fluff couscous with fork and remove herbs before serving.

❉ Lasagna ❦

If the noodles and filling are precooked, layer ingredients and cook casserole until hot and bubbly, about 1 hour. For a lasagna recipe using uncooked noodles, see, "No-boil Mexican tofu lasagna" in Chapter Fourteen: Casseroles.

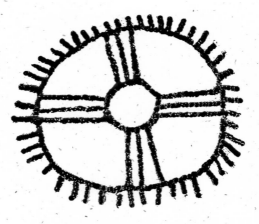

CHAPTER TEN

Sautes, roux & gravy

Basic method: Cook food in a small amount of fat at medium to high heat until lightly browned. A preheated cast iron skillet is ideal. For small amounts of food, the skillet should be left uncovered. For larger volumes of food, toss food with a little oil, cover and braise until done.

❊ Dan's cilantro salsa ❊

This recipe demonstrates the basic sautéing procedure. For a heartier salsa, add a jar of your favorite bottled salsa and omit the lime juice and jalapeno. Makes a small to large bowl of salsa depending on the amount of bottled salsa.

1 tablespoon olive or canola oil
1 bunch scallions, sliced
or ¼ cup minced onion + 2/3 cup
minced chives
1–5 cloves garlic, minced
1 red or green jalapeno chile, minced
or 1 teaspoon cracked red pepper, (optional)
5–6 plum tomatoes or 3 medium slicing tomatoes

or 3 cups cherry tomatoes, diced
½ bunch cilantro leaves, minced (optional)
1 16–32 oz jar of bottled salsa (optional)
Squeeze of ½ lime (optional)
Salt to taste

1. In a small saucepan or preheated cast iron skillet, sauté white part of scallions or ¼ cup onion, garlic and jalapeno in oil a few minutes, until onions are clear. Do not let garlic burn. If using a cast iron pan, remove pan from cooker before onions and garlic are fully cooked. The pan will continue to hold the heat for several minutes.
2. Mix ingredients in a 2-quart bowl. The salsa tastes better if the flavors are allowed to mingle for a couple of hours before serving. Refrigerate salsa up to a week.

❋ Pizza sauce ❋

This is my favorite pizza sauce. It is for garlic lovers. The fennel is the secret ingredient that makes the sauce taste like a pizzeria. It makes enough for one large 16" pizza or two or three smaller pizzas. It freezes well. In place of tomato paste, try the "Mock tomato sauce" in Chapter Thirteen: Vegetables. See solar pizza crust directions in Chapter Sixteen: Baked goods: bread, pancakes, pastries & more.

2 teaspoons olive or canola oil
5 cloves minced garlic
1 teaspoon whole fennel seeds
2 6-oz cans tomato paste
2 teaspoons dried flaked Italian herb mixture
Salt to taste

1. Sauté garlic and fennel until garlic is just barely cooked, a few minutes. Do not let the garlic burn!
2. Mix sauté with remaining ingredients. Spread on pizza, add toppings and bake.

✳ Spicy nut butter sauce ✳

This recipe is inspired by Thai peanut sauce. Try a variety of nut and seed butters, raw and roasted, for different flavors. (See Chapter Seventeen for toasting nuts). Serve over vegetables, grains, pasta, polenta or potatoes. **2–6 servings**

1 tablespoon olive or canola oil
5 cloves garlic, minced
1 bunch scallions or 1/3 cup onion, minced
1–3 teaspoons minced ginger
1–3 teaspoons chile paste or minced jalapeno (optional)
½ cup nut butter
1 tablespoon soy sauce
1 teaspoon lemon or lime juice
or a mild vinegar such as rice or cider (optional)
Vegetable broth, coconut milk or water as needed
1 teaspoon ground coriander (optional)
½ cup chopped fresh cilantro or basil (optional)

1. Sauté garlic, scallions, ginger and chiles a few minutes.
2. In a small bowl, whisk sauté into nut butter. Add soy sauce, juice or vinegar and enough broth to achieve desired consistency. Nut butter emulsifies when mixed with water. It will absorb more liquid than you might think.
3. If desired, mix in coriander and fresh herbs.

❋ Seasoned breadcrumbs ❋

Heat 1 tablespoon Earth Balance™, olive or canola oil in a covered 3-liter roaster for a few minutes. Stir in 2 cups breadcrumbs. Cover. Bake 10–20 minutes until lightly browned. Stir once for even browning.

❋ Roux, sauce and gravy ❋

A roux is a mixture of fat and flour that is used to thicken soups, stews, gumbo, white sauce or gravy. The fat should be a refined vegetable oil suitable for high temperature cooking, such as canola oil or melted Earth Balance™. Any grain or legume flour can be used to make roux. All-purpose flour is standard, but my personal favorite is garbanzo flour because it has a rich, savory flavor. If making sauce or gravy, this amount of roux will thicken 3–4 cups of liquid.

¼ cup fat
¼ cup flour

1. Heat oil in covered roaster or casserole dish.
2. Whisk in flour, let cook for a just a few minutes for a light roux, until flour begins to brown, or longer for a dark roux.
3. If making sauce or gravy with the roux, remove skillet from cooker, carefully whisk in milk or broth without splattering yourself, and place in cooker for a few minutes to thicken. Repeat whisking once or twice, as needed.

❋ Mushroom gravy ❋

Braise 8 oz sliced mushrooms in 2 teaspoons oil and 1 tablespoon soy sauce until they shrink (see Chapter 13 for details on braising vegetables). Whisk in garbanzo flour and proceed with roux recipe. Use broth or milk for liquid. Season with rosemary, marjoram, sage and thyme to taste. **2 to 4 servings**

CHAPTER ELEVEN
Soups & stews

Basic method: Mix ingredients and cooking liquid in a pot, cover, and simmer until done. If using a panel cooker, make small volumes to cut down on cooking time. Box cookers can simmer up to 8 cups of stew in a few hours.

❋ Solar soup stock ❋

Making soup stock is a good use of your cooker on days when you don't have a lot of other food to cook, as it takes several hours. Divide up and freeze for later use. For basic water heating and defrosting directions, see Chapter Six: Preheating, defrosting & melting. Use whatever flavoring ingredients you have on hand. Save scrap items such as tomato peels and chard stems in the refrigerator or freezer until needed. If desired, add extra flavor by sautéing garlic, onions and whole spices in your solar cooker before adding the rest of the ingredients. Or pre-broil vegetables in a parabolic reflector. Or roast vegetables in a conventional oven or earth oven (Chapter Twenty Three) until caramelized.

❋ Simple vegetarian broth ❋

Here's a list of my favorite stock ingredients. The mushrooms, lentils and nettles create a "meaty" flavor and rich brown color, while the carrots or tomato skins add a bright orange color and tangy flavor. The potato or grains help to thicken the broth. Lovage is a perennial garden herb in the celery family. Substitute diced celery if not available. Add a salty ingredient to help draw juices out of the plant cell walls. I use a 4-quart stock pot to make this recipe, filling the pot about one-third full of vegetables and then adding enough water to fill the pot up to about four-fifths full. **6–8 cups broth**

Onions
Whole garlic cloves
Whole dried red chile pods
Dried mushrooms
Brown lentils
Carrots or tomato peels
Dried stinging nettles
Dried lovage
Whole potato or handful of wheat berries, oats or barley
Whole coriander seeds
Whole fennel seeds
A dash of salt, tamari or miso
Fresh leafy herbs (stems OK) such as parsley, oregano, marjoram and cilantro

1. Finely dice vegetables.
2. Combine ingredients in the pot. Make sure to leave some air space on top to allow for heat circulation inside the pot.
3. Cover and simmer until vegetables are very soft and drained of color. It will take at least a couple of hours for the broth to heat to the boiling point and another hour or two of simmering time. Four hours is ideal in my Sun Oven™.
4. Strain the broth through a fine mesh strainer or a chinois, a conical, funnel-shaped strainer with a long handle, used for straining soups and sauces. Press out as much liquid as possible with a wooden pestle or the back of a large spoon.

❊ Garden minestrone ❦

This recipe is sized for a 3-liter roaster. I make minestrone from whatever seasonal vegetables, herbs, beans and grains I have on hand. Vary the proportions of ingredients as desired. Choose a rainbow of colors or stick to a color theme, such as red (i.e. tomatoes, red bell peppers and red beans). I especially like including fennel, which has a sweet anise flavor, and lovage, which has a curried celery flavor. Another excellent minestrone flavoring is a dollop of pesto added to each serving bowl. **4– 8 servings**

1 tablespoon olive or canola oil
1 medium onion, diced
1–5 cloves garlic, minced
1 cup cooked beans or lentils
½ cup dry orzo, ½ cup rinsed quinoa, 1 diced potato
or 1 cup leftover, cooked grains
2 cups mixed diced vegetables (peppers, tomatoes, winter squash, corn, etc.)
4 cups vegetable stock
1 tablespoon sweet Hungarian paprika, chile powder
or tomato paste (optional)
1 tablespoon dry Italian herb mix
Salt, tamari or miso to taste
1 cup fresh cilantro, basil or parsley, finely chopped

1. If desired, sauté onion and garlic in oil. Otherwise, skip this step and just add the oil, onion and garlic to the pot along with the rest of the vegetables.
2. Add everything except for the fresh herbs to the pot. Cover and simmer until vegetables are tender, about 3 hours. If using leafy greens, add hearty greens like kale about halfway through the cooking. Delicate greens like spinach or sorrel should not be added until Step 3.
3. Remove pot from the cooker and stir in the fresh herbs and delicate leafy greens. Adjust seasonings, let sit 10–20 minutes to cool and let flavors mingle before serving.

❉ Vegetarian posole ❦

Posole, the stew (as opposed to plain posole corn), is tradi-
tionally made with pork. Here's a vegan bean-based version.
This recipe also works great with winter squash in place of
the bell peppers, or browned seitan in place of the beans.
Basic posole cooking directions are found in Chapter Seven:
Grains, polenta & porridge. **4–8 servings**

1 tablespoon olive, canola or refined coconut oil
1 large yellow or red onion, diced
1–5 cloves minced garlic
2 bell peppers, preferably different colors, chopped
1 cup cooked white or yellow posole
1 cup cooked pinto, Anasazi or black beans
1 15-oz can diced tomatoes
or 1 ½ cups chopped fresh tomatoes
3–4 cups vegetable broth or tomato juice
1 tablespoon New Mexican chile powder (mild or hot)
2 teaspoons dried oregano
1 vegetable bouillon cube or salt to taste
½ cup fresh chopped cilantro or parsley (optional)

1. Toss the oil, onions, garlic and bell peppers and braise in a
covered 3-liter roaster until soft.
2. Add posole, beans, tomatoes, chile powder, oregano, salt
and broth. Cover and cook until heated through, about 1 hour.
3. Remove pot from cooker and stir in cilantro.

CHAPTER TWELVE
Fruit, jam & pie filling

Basic method: Cook fruit and other ingredients in a covered pot until soft. Chutney, jam and fruit butter can be stored in the refrigerator for several weeks, frozen for several months, or canned in a boiling water bath (see Chapter Eighteen: Solar pasteurization & canning).

❋ Poached fresh fruit ❋

Plums, peaches, apricots, pears, quinces, apples, cherries, figs, berries and bananas are all delicious when cooked in a solar cooker. Slice tree fruits in half. Leave cherries or berries whole. Serve alone, with ice cream, or use as a sauce for grains, oatmeal, polenta or other foods.

Cut-sides up: Place fruit cut-sides up in a single layer in the baking dish. Drizzle some sweetener over the fruit and add a pat of Earth Balance™ or coconut oil to each cavity. Cover and cook until soft.

Cut-sides down: Lightly oil a graniteware roaster or baking dish that has sides at least 1 ½ inches high. Place fruit cut-side down in a single layer in the baking dish. The following poaching sauce is optional, but adds richness: pour ½–1 inch concentrated fruit juice or wine into the pan. Melt a table-spoon or two of Earth Balance™ or coconut oil and 1 table-spoon sugar, agave syrup, maple syrup or honey and drizzle over fruit. Cook for 45 minutes–1 ½ hours, or until fruit is soft. Large apples and quinces will take longer to soften than stone fruits and berries.

❉ Dried fruit compotes and chutneys ❦

Compote is a mixture of chopped, dried fruit simmered in fruit juice with a little sweetener. Chutney is a type of compote that includes savory flavors like diced onions, ginger and vinegar for a sweet-and-sour tang. Here's a really good dried apricot chutney sized for a 3-liter graniteware roaster. **8–12 servings**

1 cup dried apricots
Enough water to cover apricots
½ cup raisins
½ cup dried apples
1 cinnamon stick
½ cup cider vinegar
¼ cup candied ginger
or 2 tablespoons minced fresh ginger
½–¾ cup brown sugar or maple sugar
(or use a liquid sweetener like agave syrup or honey
and reduce water accordingly)

1. Dice dried fruit.
2. Add apricots to pot with just enough water to cover.
If using liquid sweetener, include it during this step.
Add rest of the ingredients.
3. Cover pot and heat to the boiling point, about 1 hour. To help moisture evaporate, open lid slightly and vent the cooker. Simmer chutney another 45 minutes, or until thick and dark.

❋ Applesauce ❋

Making applesauce is easy. Core and dice enough apples to fill a cooking pot halfway. I leave the peels on mine, but you can peel if desired. Toss a little lemon juice (a teaspoon or two depending on how many apples you have) over the apples to prevent them from browning. Add 1–2 teaspoons sweetener to balance out lemon juice (dry sugar, agave syrup or honey all work great). Add additional sweetener to taste (I never do). Add ¼–½ cup apple cider or other fruit juice (prickly pear cactus juice creates a beautiful bright magenta color and adds an extra flavor dimension). If desired, add cinnamon. Cover and simmer until apples are soft, 30 minutes–1 hour or more, depending on volume. Mash or blend to desired consistency.

❋ Fruit butter ❋

Make applesauce (or poach plums, cherries, apricots or other fruit). Blend until smooth. Pour sauce back into cooking pot and add sugar and spices as desired (cinnamon, cloves and nutmeg are popular flavorings for fruit butters). Place back in cooker with a slightly uncovered lid, vent cooker and simmer until butter is reduced in volume by about half. This will take several hours to all day long, depending on the volume of ingredients and the temperature of the cooker.

❋ Pumpkin butter ❋

Bake and mash a winter squash, preferably
a deep orange variety like butternut or
kabocha. Proceed as for fruit butter.
Because squash/pumpkin is a low
acid vegetable, it *cannot* be canned
in a boiling water bath like fruit
butter (See Chapter Eighteen).
Refrigerate up to 2 weeks or
freeze up to 1 year.

❋ Fruit jam or syrup ❋

*Use this recipe with whole berries, cherries or diced tree fruit.
To remove seeds from raspberries and other fruit, run the fruit
through a food mill before simmering. Very ripe fruits such as
peaches may not need added sweetener. Tart wild berries may
need up to an equal volume of sugar. Dry sugar will create jam
while liquid sweeteners will create syrup. You can make larger
quantities, but the pot will take several hours to bring to a boil.*

**1 ½ cups fresh or frozen fruit
2 tablespoons –1 ½ cups dry sugar or liquid sweetener
(agave syrup, maple syrup or honey)**

1. Mix fruit and sugar in 3-liter graniteware roaster.
2. Cook 30–45 minutes, until thickened.

❋ Precooked pie filling ❋

Precooked pie filling is recommended for solar pies. Keep fruit
whole or in recognizable slices. For a 9-inch pie, cook 1 quart
of fruit, ½ cup fruit juice and 2 tablespoons cornstarch or
arrowroot powder. Pour filling into partially baked pie shell
and finish baking pie until crust is lightly browned. Or pour
filling into a fully baked pie shell and allow to gel before serving (See Chapter Sixteen for pie crust directions).

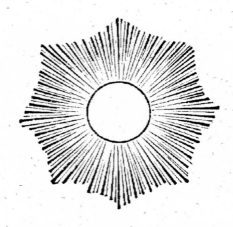

CHAPTER THIRTEEN
Vegetables

Basic method: In a covered pot, braise, steam or bake until tender. In amny cases, no added liquid is necessary. The low to moderate temperatures of solar box and panel cookers retain the colors and vitamins of vegetables.

❄ Braised vegetables ❄

The easiest way to cook vegetables is to braise them in their own juices: In humid climates or if using a single reflector box cooker or a panel cooker, added water is not necessary. In arid climates, add ¼–½ inch water. You can also toss vegetables with 1 tablespoon olive oil before braising.

The cooking time for whole root vegetables like beets, carrots and turnips, and "above ground" veggies like asparagus, green beans, eggplant and artichokes varies according to their volume. For example, three whole medium beets or a bunch of whole carrots cook in about an hour. A large pot of vegetables will take several hours to cook.

❋ Steamed vegetables ❦

Use a steamer insert like on a stovetop.
Preheat ¾ inch water before adding veggies.
Cover and steam until tender. Veggies can
also be steamed on top of simmering grain.
The cooking time is approximately the same
as for stovetop steaming.

❋ Whole winter squash ❦

Bake in a covered roaster with ¼ inch
water. A medium butternut, kabocha
or spaghetti squash will take
about 2 hours to become tender,
while a large squash requires at
least 3 hours.

❋ Whole potatoes ❦

Add ¼ inch water to cooking pot, add potatoes and bake.
Potatoes are very dense. They take a long time to heat up. 2
lbs potatoes will become fork-tender in about 1 ½ hours if the
cooker if fully preheated. If you want lightly browned skin
and an "oven-baked" flavor, vent cooker and pot and bake
until potato skin is lightly browned and crispy.

❋ Garlicky mashed potatoes ❦

Quarter several baking potatoes and place in a roaster. Cover
potatoes with water or broth. Add several whole garlic cloves
and a pinch of salt. The garlic becomes very mild in flavor, so
add more than you would normally use
in other situations. Cover. Simmer until
potatoes are soft, at least 1 ½ hours. Drain
and mash potatoes and garlic with a little
flax/hemp/olive oil or Earth Balance™.

❧ Roasted winter vegetables ❦

Toss 4–6 cups sliced, mixed root vegetables and winter squash with 2–3 tablespoons olive or canola oil, a few teaspoons aromatic herbs such as minced rosemary or an Italian mix, and salt to taste. Another good addition is 2–3 tablespoons maple or agave syrup. Bake 2–3 hours. Partway through cooking, loosen lid and vent cooker to lightly caramelize vegetables.

❧ Mock tomato sauce ❦

This magenta-red sauce tastes remarkably like tomato sauce. I served pizza to my husband, a confirmed beet hater. He ate three huge pieces, asking, "Why is this sauce so pink?".

1 part cooked beets
2–3 parts cooked winter squash with deep orange flesh

1. Peel cooked beets; their skins will slip right off.
2. Scoop out squash flesh.
3. Blend beets and squash in a food processor or blender. Leave slightly chunky or blend until smooth, as desired.

❧ Blanched tomatoes and peppers ❦

Cook 3 whole tomatoes or bell peppers in their own juices for 30 minutes. Rinse briefly under cold water and slip off skins. For fully cooked tomatoes or peppers, cook 1 hour, until soft.

❧ Corn on the cob ❦

Cook whole ears of corn in a covered roaster either husked, or with husks still attached. Estimate cooking time at roughly 20 minutes per ear. If desired, presoak cobs in salted water before roasting as is done before grilling to impart extra flavor.

❋ Steamed leafy greens and peas ❋

Be careful not to overcook greens and peas; overcooked greens and peas will turn an unappetizing olive green color and leafy greens will dry to a crisp in dry climates. Leafy greens can be stuffed into a steamer up to the lid — they'll wilt very quickly. Cook tender greens and peas 5–10 minutes. Tough greens like kale take longer.

❋ Garden ratatouille ❋

Use this basic template for other thick vegetable stews, such as Ethiopian tagines or coconut milk-based Asian dishes.

1. Chop a mixture of seasonal summer vegetables, such as eggplant, tomatoes, peppers, green beans, zucchini, corn, and baby root vegetables. Make them the same size so they will cook evenly. Add a diced onion and some minced garlic. If desired, first sauté onion in a little oil.

2. Fill cooking pot about half-way with vegetables. Cooked beans or seitan cubes are other good additions. Add sprigs of fresh herbs (especially good: rosemary, basil, parsley, oregano, thyme) or a couple of teaspoons of dried, flaked herbs, and salt to taste. Pour in an inch of vegetable broth and a tablespoon or two of tomato paste or paprika.

3. Cover. Stew until vegetables are soft, 1–3 hours depending on volume. Stir once or twice to evenly distribute ingredients.

4. After cooking, add fresh minced herbs such as basil, chives, oregano, parsley or cilantro, if desired.

✳ Glazed root vegetables ✳

Glazing works with all root vegetables. The following sweeteners are especially good: agave syrup, maple syrup, honey, apricot jam, orange marmalade or dry sugar. In place of the fennel, try other aromatic spices like orange zest or fresh minced rosemary. Another variation is to leave out the spices and add wet or dry mustard along with the sweetener. You can also use precooked vegetables and skip the first step below.

6–8 servings

**1 lb carrots, sliced into sticks 2" long x ½ to ½ inch thick
(or choose another root vegetable)
1 cup vegetable broth
½ teaspoon whole fennel seeds
A splash of lemon or lime juice or cider vinegar
Salt to taste
1 tablespoon oil
2 teaspoons dry sugar, liquid sweetener or fruit jam**

1. In a 3-liter pot, mix the carrots, broth, fennel, juice or vinegar and salt. Cover and simmer until the carrots are mostly cooked, about 20 minutes.

2. Remove pot from cooker. Stir in oil and sweetener. Place pot back in cooker uncovered. Vent cooker slightly and simmer until most of the liquid has evaporated, which will take up an hour, depending on the temperature of the cooker. Remove from cooker and stir to evenly distribute the glaze.

❊ Caramelized onions ❊

Caramelized onions are sweet and juicy, perfect as a side dish, as a topping for grains, or add to soups and stews. Dice yellow or white onions into ½ inch pieces (4 large onions fit into a 3-liter graniteware roaster). Grease the bottom of roaster with olive or canola oil and spread onions in an even layer. Bake 4 hours, stirring about once an hour to prevent tops from burning, until onions have turned a rich medium brown color. To make a smooth spread, blend with whole garlic cloves.

❊ Veggie stir-fry with tofu, ❊ tempeh or seitan

Coat the bottom of a roaster with 1 tablespoon oil. First cook the ingredients with the longest cooking times, such as root vegetables. Stir to coat veggies with oil, add a splash of soy sauce or pinch of salt and cook about 20 minutes, until half-cooked. Add vegetables with a medium cooking time, such as garlic, mushrooms and zucchini, as well as diced, precooked tofu, tempeh or seitan. Cook another 20 minutes until those foods are nearly done. Add delicate leafy greens and peas and cook briefly until wilted or tender.

CHAPTER FOURTEEN
Casseroles & one pot meals

Basic method: Layer ingredients in covered casserole dish and bake until bubbly and tender. For fast cooking, size for a 3-liter graniteware roaster. For larger dishes, use a 9" x 13" baking dish. Depending on volume, baking takes 1–4 hours.

❈ One pot meal ❈

It's easy to cook a nutritious and tasty one-pot meal or casse-role dish in a solar box or panel cooker. Casseroles include lasagna, enchiladas, bread stuffing, scalloped vegetables, gratins, cabbage rolls and stuffed vegetables.

For a simple one pot meal, include a dry grain or small pasta and it's cooking liquid, some precooked beans or cubed tofu, tempeh or seitan, and seasonal vegetables. Because vegetables cook faster than grains, they should be left in large pieces, for example, whole carrots or halved bell peppers. Add delicate vegetables like peas and leafy greens in the last 15 minutes or so of cooking. Cook casserole until grains or pasta are done.

❊ Scalloped potatoes ❊

Use the cooking tips in this recipe to make all kinds of scalloped dishes and gratins. The trick to making thick creamy scalloped vegetables and cheesy gratins in a solar cooker is to precook both the vegetables and the white sauce. This recipe requires a 9" x 13" covered casserole dish. If using a 3-liter graniteware roaster, halve the recipe. Precook potatoes whole in the morning or the day before you bake the casserole. I like to leave the skins on. I prefer to use garbanzo flour to make the roux for extra flavor and nutrition. **12–16 servings**

2 lb cooked baking potatoes, preferably Yukon Gold
or Yellow Finn (4–6 medium)
3 tablespoons Earth Balance™, olive or canola oil
¼ cup garbanzo flour, whole wheat pastry flour
or all-purpose flour
1 cup nondairy milk + 1 bouillon cube
(or use dry soy milk powder mixed with vegetable broth)
Garlic or onion salt to taste
2 oz cheese, grated (I use VeganRella™)
½ cup mayonnaise (I use vegan Vegenaise™)
1 cup dry breadcrumbs

1. Peel potatoes if desired and slice into ¼ inch-thick slices.
2. If necessary, dissolve the bouillon cube in the milk. Make roux and white sauce with milk and garlic or onion salt. After sauce is thickened, remove from cooker and stir in cheese and mayonnaise. Gently mix sauce into potatoes.
3. Spread ingredients evenly in a greased casserole dish. Sprinkle bread crumbs on top.
4. Cover and cook 1 ½ hours, or until bread crumbs become lightly browned.

❋ No-boil Mexican tofu lasagna ❋

This recipe is my husband's favorite dish. It includes Mexican and Asian influences. The lasagna noodles do not require pre-cooking — they soften right in the sauce. I prefer to freeze the tofu for at least a couple of weeks to produce a firmer, chewier texture (See Chapter Fifteen for tofu prep directions).
12–16 servings

12 oz firm or extra firm water-packed tofu
1 tablespoon olive or canola oil
2–4 minced garlic cloves
8 oz sliced mushrooms
1 small red or green bell pepper, diced
½ bunch leafy greens
(kale, collards, spinach, chard, beet greens) shredded
2 tablespoons soy sauce
2 6-oz cans tomato paste
2 15-oz cans red enchilada sauce (mild, medium or hot)
2 teaspoons dried Italian herb mixture
or ¼ cup minced fresh oregano
3 enchilada cans worth of water or vegetable broth
1 8-oz package cheese (I use VeganRella™)
12 uncooked lasagna noodles

1. In a covered pot, pour in oil and rotate bottom to coat. Add garlic, bell pepper and mushrooms. Drizzle with soy sauce and stir to combine. Cover and braise for 20 minutes, until mushrooms begin to shrink. In a bowl, crumble the tofu and drizzle in another tablespoon of soy sauce. Stir the tofu into the vegetables (and if using fresh oregano, add it now, too). Cover and cook another 20 minutes. Add greens to pot, cover, and cook 10–20 minutes until wilted. Remove pot from cooker, stir to mix and set aside.
2. While the vegetables are cooking, grate the cheese. In a 2-quart bowl whisk together tomato paste, enchilada sauce, dry herbs and water or broth to make a sauce of soupy consistency.
3. Assemble lasagna in a 9" x 13" inch covered casserole dish: Ladle a ½-inch layer of sauce into bottom of pan and

add 1/3 cup water or broth. Arrange 3 noodles across the bottom, placing a fourth noodle horizontally across the end. Spoon half of the vegetable-tofu mixture evenly over the surface and sprinkle about 3 oz cheese. Ladle enough sauce over the surface of the casserole to barely cover filling layer. Repeat with a second layer of noodles, tofu mixture, cheese and sauce. Place the last 4 noodles on top. Pour the remaining sauce over the top. If there is not enough sauce to coat the noodles with at least 1/8 inch of sauce, pour in some extra water or broth to cover. Sprinkle remaining cheese across top.

4. Cover pan with a dark lid and bake 2 ½ hours, or until noodles are fully cooked.

5. Remove lasagna from cooker. Uncover and cool for at least 10–15 minutes before serving to allow the lasagna to gel a bit. A full hour allows the texture to firm up and the flavors to mingle. Once fully cooled, refrigerate uneaten portion. The lasagna is better on the second day after it has fully firmed up and the flavors have mingled.

❋ Defrosting and reheating casseroles ❊

Heating a 9" x 13" lasagna made with preboiled noodles or reheating a refrigerated casserole in a box or panel cooker takes 1–2 hours, depending on the oven temperature. One serving takes only 15 minutes. If the casserole is frozen when placed in the cooker, it will take about 4 hours to heat up, or all day using the absentee cooking method. See Chapter Six: Preheating, defrosting & melting for more information.

CHAPTER FIFTEEN
Tofu, tempeh, seitan & veggie burgers

Basic method: Slice tofu, tempeh, seitan, or veggie burgers into ½–¾ inch thick slabs or cubes. Cover and steam or bake until done. It is also possible to barbeque in a solar cooker and to cook whole frozen tofu roasts.

❋ Steamed tofu or tempeh ❋

2–4 servings

Tempeh and water-packed tofu should never be eaten raw. Tempeh contains a fermentation inoculant that must be thoroughly cooked before using secondary cooking methods like roasting and baking. Tofu is not sterile unless sealed in aseptic packaging. Dice 8 oz tempeh or tofu and cook in a casserole dish or roaster with 2 tablespoons water or insert a steamer and add ¾ inch of water. Cover and heat water until steaming. Add tofu or tempeh and cook 20 minutes.

❄ Marinated tofu, tempeh ❦ or seitan cutlets

2–4 servings

8 oz tofu, tempeh or seitan, sliced into ½ inch thick cutlets
Broth or water as needed
2–3 tablespoons soy sauce or tamari
1 tablespoon lemon or lime juice
5 cloves minced garlic, or to taste
2 teaspoons sliced or minced ginger
1 tablespoon toasted sesame oil (optional)
2 teaspoons fresh minced chile
or cracked red pepper flakes (optional)

1. Arrange cutlets in a single layer in a casserole dish.
2. Mix marinade ingredients and pour over slabs, adding just enough broth or water to cover. Marinate at least 45 minutes, or up to two days refrigerated. Once or twice, turn over the slabs for even marinating.
2. Bake cutlets in a single layer on a greased, covered cookie sheet or casserole until firm and lightly browned, about 1 ½ hours.

Tofu prep

I prefer very firm tofu in most dishes. I usually freeze and thaw extra firm tofu before using. Freezing changes the texture of tofu, making it firmer and spongier and better able to soak up the cooking flavors. Tofu can also be pressed to drain off excess water before cooking between cloths or paper towels and weighted down with a baking tray and some cans of food or rocks for 30 minutes.

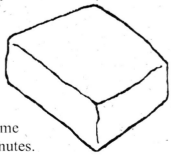

❋ Simmered seitan ❦

If you knead seitan from scratch or use instant gluten, simmer the raw dough in your solar cooker. Slice into 1"-diameter cubes. In a 3-liter or larger roaster, submerge cubes in cold broth (this creates a firmer texture), cover and heat until boiling. Simmer 1 hour. Let cool to room temperature in the broth.

❋ Scrambled tofu ❦

Coat bottom of 3-liter roaster with 1 tablespoon oil. Add 1 lb crumbled tofu (I do it by hand right over the pot), some minced garlic or garlic powder, a squirt of soy sauce and other flavorings like nutritional yeast, tumeric (for bright yellow color), oregano, or finely minced vegetables. Mix ingredients, cover and cook until tofu is steaming hot and the vegetables are tender, about 20 minutes. **3–4 servings**

❋ Glazed tofu, tempeh or seitan ❦

Use the glazed root vegetable recipe in Chapter Thirteen. Substitute precooked tofu, tempeh or seitan cubes.

❋ Browned tofu, tempeh or seitan ❦

To make crispy cubes of tofu, tempeh or seitan, you need to preheat a cast iron skillet or tortilla pan. When the pan is ready, dice 8 oz tofu, tempeh or seitan into ½ inch cubes. Drizzle 2 teaspoons of olive or canola oil and 2 teaspoons of soy sauce over the cubes and mix to evenly spread the soy sauce across their surfaces. Spread the cubes on the skillet and cover with an overturned 3-liter black graniteware pot. Tofu and precooked seitan brown in 20–25 minutes at 300°F/ 149°C, while tempeh browns in 40–45 minutes. You can also bake the cubes like marinated cutlets, but they won't get as crispy. Toss browned cubes into stir fries, pilafs, marinated salads or use as a pizza topping.

❋ Barbequed tofu, tempeh or seitan ❦

I like to make this recipe with Chinese style seitan. This technique also works for other types of thick sauces, such as yogurt-based tandoori-style marinades. **2 to 8 servings**

8–16 oz pressed tofu, pre-steamed tempeh,
or raw or cooked seitan
Salt water or soy sauce-based marinade (for tempeh)
½–1 cup barbeque sauce

1. Slice tofu, tempeh or seitan into square or rectangular slabs ¼–½ inch thick, or into cubes. Marinate tempeh in a salty broth for 2 hours to infuse the salt throughout the pieces.
2. Coat each piece with barbeque sauce and arrange on a lightly greased 9" x 13" baking pan or larger cookie sheet.
3. Loosely cover pan and bake 2–2 ½ hours, until sauce thickens and begins to caramelize and the tofu, tempeh or seitan is firm. For even browning, flip pieces halfway through.

❋ Veggie burgers ❦

Heat up prepared frozen veggie/tempeh burgers for 30 minutes on a lightly greased, uncovered cast iron skillet or dark cookie sheet to make them crispy. Flip over halfway through cooking. Homemade burgers and patties are cooked the same way, but the baking pan should be loosely covered with another pan or lid and baked up to 2 hours or more, until lightly browned.

❋ Solar vegan roast ❦

Place a frozen Tofurky™ or other precooked vegan roast in a covered pot and heat until defrosted, about 2 hours. Once defrosted, you can baste the roast with a savory marinade (try soy sauce, fruit juice and a little sweetener), if desired. Bake another 2 hours, or until it begins to brown.

CHAPTER SIXTEEN

Baked goods: breads, muffins, pancakes, cookies, pies & more

Basic method: Baking raw dough requires clear, sunny skies between 10 a.m. and 2 p.m., especially during fall, winter and spring. Unless otherwise specified, loosely cover baking pan and vent cooker to release excess moisture. Baked goods will lightly brown. Box cookers perform better than panel cookers.

❋ Yeast bread basics ❋

Solar-baked yeast breads have a thin, lightly browned crust and fluffy crumb.

- **Pans:** Cover yeast breads during baking. A 1–1 ½ lb loaf fits perfectly in a 3-liter graniteware roaster. Or spraypaint two loaf pans black, and turn one upside down on top of the other. Gray nonstick and dark glass bread pans also work. Don't fill pan more than 1/3 full with unproofed dough, or there won't be enough air space to hold the steam.
- **Baking:** Bake 1 lb dough (any shape) for about one hour, until lightly browned. A fully cooked loaf reaches 190-210°F/88-99°C at its center.

❈ Dinner rolls ❦

Solar cookers make especially light, fluffy rolls. For the last proofing, shape 1 lb dough into 6–12 balls. Lightly oil them and arrange in a 3-liter graniteware roaster. Bake about 1 hour.

❈ Sweet rolls ❦

½ lb of dough makes enough rolls to fit a 3-liter graniteware roaster. 1 lb fills a 9" x 13" baking dish. Split dough into 2–3 sections; roll out to less than ¼ inch thick. Spread with fillings. Roll into a log and slice into 1–1 ½ inch thick spirals.

❈ Pizza and focaccia ❦

Flatten ½ lb dough (made with about 2 cups flour) in a 9" x 13" casserole dish. If making focaccia, sprinkle on toppings and bake. If making pizza, pre-bake crust without toppings until lightly browned. Spread toppings, loosely cover and bake until toppings are cooked and cheese is melted, 30 minutes to 1 hour, depending on whether the toppings are precooked or raw.

❈ Frozen bread dough ❦

To bake with frozen bread dough, you need not defrost it first. Arrange frozen loaves or rolls in greased pan, cover, and place in an unheated cooker aimed towards the sun. As the cooker heats up, the dough will defrost, rise and bake. 1 ½ lb dinner rolls takes only 1 hour and 30–45 minutes from freezer to cooling rack, depending on whether you want a fluffy crust or a crispy brown crust. Breadsticks take less time. Large loaves take 2–3 hours.

❋ Solar crackers ❋

Make crackers when the humidity is low. The following recipe is sized to fit on one medium baking tray. Multiply the volume as desired. **2–3 servings**

2 tablespoons whole wheat, spelt or unbleached flour
1/4 cup kamut, rye, garbanzo, quinoa or amaranth flour
¼ teaspoon baking powder
1 tablespoon vegetable oil or melted Earth Balance™
A few tablespoons of water, as needed
Kosher or regular salt to taste
1 tablespoon poppy or sesame seeds (optional)

1. Mix flour and baking powder.
2. Stir in oil. Add just enough water to make a stiff dough.
3. Lightly dust a wooden board with flour and roll out the dough to less than 1/8 inch thick. Sprinkle with the salt and seeds, pressing them lightly into the dough. Use a fluted pastry wheel or non-serrated knife to slice into 1–2" squares.
4. Arrange crackers so they don't touch each other on a dark, lightly greased baking sheet. Bake uncovered or cover loosely with an overturned baking tray or piece of black cloth. Vent the cooker to allow excess moisture to escape. Bake about an hour, or until lightly browned. If using a multiple reflector cooker, do not let them burn! Cool on a cooling rack completely before storing to maintain their crispness.

❋ Indian chapatti flatbread ❋

This method also works for tortillas and other flatbreads. Use a preheated cast iron skillet or tortilla griddle. **2–4 servings**

1 cup whole wheat, spelt or unbleached all-purpose flour
¼ teaspoon salt
1 teaspoon–1 tablespoon olive or canola oil, nut butter or melted EarthBalance™ or coconut oil (optional)
1/3–½ cup water

1. Mix dry ingredients in bowl.
2. Combine liquids in separate bowl and stir into dry ingredients, stirring as little as possible to combine. Slowly stir liquids into flour mixture until too stiff to stir with a fork.
3. Briefly knead dough with hands until a smooth ball forms. Cover with a damp cloth and let rest 30 minutes.
4. Roll individual pieces of dough into 1/16–¼-inch thick rounds. Pat, roll or press into final shape.
5. Lightly grease skillet. Bake one flatbread at a time, covered with an overturned black roaster. Cook first side for about 5 minutes. No brown spots will appear. Flip over and cook another 5 minutes. Don't overcook or you'll get crackers.

✳ Crepes and Ethiopian injera ✳

Crepes require a preheated cast iron skillet or tortilla griddle. Tef is the favored grain for making Ethiopian injera. Turn any pancake or muffin batter into crepes by blending with extra liquid to make a pour batter the consistency of thick cream. Multiply volumes as desired. **1 serving**

¼ cup tef, quinoa, amaranth, wheat or other grain flour
¼–1/3 cup water, as needed
Pinch salt (optional)

1. Whisk flour and water in a bowl. Cover and let sit for a bare minimum of 30 minutes to allow starches to absorb the water. Longer is better. For sourdough injera, let the batter sit 24–48 hours to ferment with naturally occurring wild yeasts and lactic acid bacteria. Whisk a couple of times a day to aerate batter.
2. Before cooking, add salt and more liquid, if needed.
3. Grease cast iron skillet. Pour a thin layer of batter into skillet in a spiral pattern, beginning at the center and moving outwards. Grip skillet handle and rotate pan to even out batter.
4. Cook one crepe at a time, following directions for chapattis.

❋ Make-your-own muffins ❋

Experiment with different flavors — apple, pumpkin, corn-bread, raisin bread, etc. This recipe makes 6–8 regular sized muffins. Mini-muffin pans, corn stick pans, muffin top pans and preheated cast iron scone pans are good options, too. Sweeteners, fat and other liquids should total about 1 cup.

1 ½ cups whole wheat, spelt, rye, or unbleached flour
1 ½ teaspoons baking powder
¼ teaspoon salt
¼ teaspoon baking soda
2 tablespoons –½ cup agave syrup, maple syrup or honey
0–¼ cup canola oil or melted Earth Balance™
or coconut oil or 2–4 tablespoons ground flax seeds
or up to ½ cup nut butter
0–1 cup liquid (milk, yogurt, water, juice, applesauce,
or mashed pumpkin)
½ cup chopped dried fruit, vegetables, nuts or seeds
(optional)
1–2 teaspoons cinnamon, vanilla, maple flavoring
or other flavoring extract (optional)

1. Mix the dry and wet ingredients separately, then combine. If necessary, add enough additional liquid to make a medium drop batter.
2. Pour into greased and floured muffin cups or cupcake liners. Cover muffin tin and bake in preheated cooker about 45 minutes, or until muffins are lightly browned.

❋ Crispy cornbread ❋

For thin, crispy-style cornbread, bake batter in a greased, cov-ered 9" pie plate or graniteware roaster until lightly browned, about 45 minutes. Or bake in a preheated cast iron cornbread or cornstick pan.

❋ Steamed breads and cakes ❋

Any quick bread or cake recipe can be steamed instead of baked. Steamed breads work well in solar cookers, since they cook at the boiling point of water. They don't require added fat because they are naturally moist. Recipes made with 1 ½ cups flour fit in a 1-quart bundt pan or three 15-oz tin cans. Choose a pot for steaming that comfortably fits your cake pan or tin cans. Here's a Boston brown bread recipe. **6–8 servings**

½ cup whole wheat
or unbleached flour
½ cup cornmeal
½ cup rye flour
¼ teaspoon salt
¼ teaspoon baking soda
1 ½–1 ¾ teaspoons baking powder
½ cup molasses or other liquid sweetener
½ cup raisins or walnuts (optional)

1. Add 1 inch water to the pot and insert metal trivet. Cover and preheat until water boils.
2. Mix batter and pour into oiled and semolina-dusted cake pan or tin cans. Tightly cover with foil and a rubber band or string.
3. Place covered bread pan onto trivet. Cover and bake 2 ½–3 hours depending on your altitude. No peeking! You do not want the temperature to drop.

❋ Pancakes ❋

Any muffin recipe can be thinned with extra liquid to make pancake batter. If you have a large box cooker, pour 4–6 individual pancakes on greased baking sheet. Otherwise, make one big pancake in a 9" pie pan or granite-ware roaster. Cover and bake 30 minutes for smaller pancakes or 1 hour for a large one.

❋ Pumpkin cookies ❋

Bake solar cookies uncovered on a black or dark grey baking sheet. You can also bake cookies in a muffin tin or thin for pancakes. **12 moist, cake-textured cookies**

1 cup whole wheat pastry, spelt, rye or all-purpose flour
¼ teaspoon baking soda
¼ teaspoon baking powder
1 teaspoon cinnamon (optional)
2 tablespoons canola oil or melted unrefined coconut oil or Earth Balance™ (or use more mashed squash instead)
¾ cup mashed winter squash (I prefer kabocha)
¼ cup maple syrup, agave syrup or honey
1 teaspoon vanilla, maple flavoring or orange zest (optional)
½ cup chopped nuts, raisins or chocolate chips
Water (if needed)

1. Mix dry ingredients and set aside.
2. In a separate bowl, use a fork to blend oil, squash, sweetener and flavoring extract until smooth. Fold in nuts/raisins/chips.
3. Gently mix wet and dry ingredients until just combined. The mixture should be a stiff drop batter. If too dry, add a little liquid, if too wet, a little flour.
4. On greased baking sheet, drop batter in 3 x 4 arrangement.
5. Bake 30–40 minutes.

❋ Solar scones & biscuits ❋

This technique works for American-style baking powder biscuits, drop biscuits and scones. Roll or pat dough ¼–1 inch thick. Slice biscuits by pressing down straight with a knife (avoid sawing edges). Place biscuits upside down on an ungreased cookie sheet for a taller, lighter rise. For a soft texture, arrange just touching. For a crispier texture, leave ½ inch between biscuits. Cover and bake 30-45 minutes.

❋ Solar brownies ❦

Chocolate baked goods do not need to be covered because of their dark color. In the following recipe, the baking powder creates a dense cake-like texture. For a fudgier texture, leave it out. You can also bake this batter as drop cookies. If you use the full ½ cup of cocoa and decide the brownies aren't sweet enough for you, add ½ teaspoon powdered stevia extract to the dry ingredients. **6–12 brownies**

1 ½ cups whole pastry or unbleached all-purpose flour
¼–½ cup cocoa powder
¼ cup dry milk powder
(optional — I use Better Than Milk™ soy milk powder)
1 teaspoon baking powder (optional)
¼ teaspoon salt
½ cup canola oil or melted coconut oil or Earth Balance™
½ cup agave syrup, maple syrup or honey
1 teaspoon vanilla or maple flavoring
¾ cup chopped pecans or walnuts
1–2 tablespoons water if needed

1. Mix the dry ingredients and set aside.
2. In a second bowl, mix the oil, sweetener and flavoring extract.
3. Combine dry and wet ingredients, stirring as little as possible. If you use ½ cup cocoa and the milk powder, add 1–2 tablespoons water to make a thick pour batter. Fold in nuts.
4. Pour batter into a lightly greased 3-liter roaster and bake 45 minutes to an hour depending on whether you want a fudgier or cakier texture).

❋ Solar layer cakes ❦

Bake individual cake layers in a covered, 3-liter graniteware roaster or 9" x 13" baking dish. Bake 45 minutes or until fully cooked in the center.

❊ Make-your-own pot pie ❊

Any biscuit, scone, cornbread or pie crust dough can be used to top savory pot pies, such as thick stew, chili, and leftover mixed vegetables mixed with gravy. Don't fill the baking dish more than halfway with vegetables. A 9" x 13" casserole requires about 2 cups of sauce. Drop blobs of dough or batter on top or lay pie crust dough across surface. If necessary, cut several slits for steam to escape. Bake until filling is bubbling and crust is lightly browned, about 2 hours.

❊ Any fruit cobbler ❊

Any biscuit, scone, cornbread or pie crust dough can be used to top a fruit cobbler, too. **4–8 servings**

3–4 cups sliced fruit or whole cherries
¼ cup liquid sweetener or up to 2 cups granulated sugar
1 recipe dough topping made with 1 1/2–2 cups flour

1. Mix fruit and sweetener and spread in a lightly greased a 3-liter graniteware roaster.
2. Drop batter in tablespoon-sized lumps evenly across fruit.
3. Cover and bake 1 hour, or until scones are lightly browned and fruit juices are bubbling.

❊ Open face pies and pastries ❊

Solar cookers are best suited to open-face pies with partially or fully prebaked crusts. Lattice and crumble toppings are also good. Cover and bake an empty crust for 45 minutes–1 hour, until lightly browned. Add filling, cover and bake until filling is set. The baking time for double-crust pies is significantly longer. Bake open-face tarts and turnovers like stuffed pasta (Chapter Nine: Pasta & dumplings).

❊ Delicate nut crust ❊

Nut flour crusts bake faster than grain crusts. This crust is perfect for a precooked filling, such as (tofu) cream pie, sliced fresh fruit or cooked fruit fillings. Bake crusts made with graham crackers, sugar cookies or granola the same way.

2 ½ cups raw almond, hazelnut or pecan meal
1/3 cup granulated sugar (sucanat, turbinado
or other natural sugars work fine)
4 tablespoons melted Earth Balance™ or coconut oil

1. Mix ingredients and press into 9" pie plate. Refrigerate 30 minutes before baking.
2. Cover, bake 25 minutes. Don't let burn! Cool before filling.

❊ Apple mesquite crumble ❊

Order molasses-flavored mesquite pod flour, a native of the Southwest, from the nonprofit seedbank Native Seeds/SEARCH (www.nativeseeds.org). Slice apples less than ¼-inch thick for faster solar cooking. Softer fruits can be left in bigger slices.
4–8 servings

3–4 cups sliced apples, other tree fruit or whole cherries
2 tablespoons–2 cups sugar (depending on tartness
of fruit and personal preference)
½ cup mesquite flour
¼ cup granulated sugar (optional)
1 teaspoon cinnamon (optional)
1 cup chopped pecans
¼ cup canola oil or melted Earth Balance™ or coconut oil

1. Mix fruit and sweetener and spread in a lightly greased 3-liter graniteware roaster.
2. Mix together the flour and oil and sugar and cinnamon if using and crumble over the fruit.
3. Cover and bake 1 ½ hours until topping is lightly browned.

CHAPTER SEVENTEEN

Toasting nuts, seeds, granola & more

Basic method: Toasting is best done on days with low humidity. Spread food in a single layer across a dark baking tray. Bake uncovered or loosely covered until it browns or dries out. If you have a multiple reflector oven, do not let food burn! Cool food fully before storing to maintain crispness.

❈ Toasted grains ❈

Dry toasting grains until lightly browned produces a fluffier, nutty-flavored dish perfect for pilafs and casseroles. You can toast up to 6 cups of dry grain at once, depending on the size of your solar cooker.

1. Make sure grains are completely dry before toasting. Wet grains will begin to swell and cook, instead of brown.
2. Pour grain into a baking pan. Shake the pan to spread the grain evenly across the surface, or use a spatula for spreading. The grain should be no more than ½-inch thick
3. Bake 20 minutes. Stir. Bake another 15 minutes–1 hour. Stir every 10–20 minutes (the hotter the temperature, the more frequently the grain must be stirred). Toast until grains have a

nutty aroma and a slightly deeper shade of color. If the grain starts to smell burnt, it has been toasted too long.

4. Simmer immediately or cool and store for several days in a tightly covered container.

❋ Roasted nuts ❋

Good nuts for roasting include almonds, hazelnuts, pecans, pine nuts, walnuts, and sunflower seeds. If you are mixing several kinds of nuts and seeds, chop the larger nuts so that they are roughly the same size as the smaller ones. Spread a single layer of nuts on a baking tray and toast uncovered until lightly browned, about 20 minutes. Stir at least once during the middle of the baking time to ensure even browning.

❋ Maple nuts ❋

4 cups (1 lb) raw nuts
2 teaspoons–¼ cup canola oil or melted Earth Balance™ or coconut oil
¾ cup maple syrup, agave syrup or honey
½ teaspoon salt (optional)
½ teaspoon cinnamon or grated orange zest (optional)

1. Mix the fat, sweetener, salt and spices in a bowl that is large enough to mix the nuts. Add the nuts and stir to coat with the liquid.

2. If using 2 teaspoons fat, grease baking tray. Roast nuts 20–30 minutes, or until the coating dries out. Watch carefully. You do not want to let them brown or burn.

3. Remove tray from oven and allow nuts to cool (or pour onto parchment paper to cool). Break up the nuts (they will be stuck together) and store in an airtight container in a cool, dry place for up to a couple of weeks.

❊ Tamari nuts ❊

Pour nuts, sunflower or pumpkin seeds into a bowl. Squirt tamari over the nuts to lightly coat. Spread nuts evenly in a single layer on a baking tray. Toast until lightly browned.

❊ Toasted seeds ❊

For small seeds such as hemp seeds, sesame seeds and poppy seeds, preheat baking tray or graniteware roaster. Pour in a single layer of seeds. Shake tray to evenly distribute the seeds. Bake uncovered for a few minutes. If seeds are not yet done, shake and bake another few minutes.

❊ Toasted spices ❊

Whole spices like cumin, coriander and mustard seeds and small dried chiles can be dry toasted before adding them whole or ground to Indian curries, Southwestern chili recipes, or other spicy dishes. Toasting changes their flavor and makes them easier to grind in a mortar and pestle. Toast just like other seeds. If toasted too long, spices develop a bitter flavor.

❊ Garbanzo "nuts" ❊

Garbanzo nuts are a popular Italian snack food. Toss 1 cup cooked garbanzo beans with 2 teaspoons oil and a pinch of salt or soy sauce to taste. Spread beans in a single layer on a greased baking tray. Bake uncovered until lightly brown and crispy, at least 1 ½ hours. Other beans can be toasted, too. Toasted beans are good in salads, pilafs and stews.

❈ Make-your-own granola ❦

2 cups mixed ingredients: rolled or flaked grains, chopped nuts or seeds, flaked coconut, dried fruit, wheat germ and ground flax seeds
¼ cup liquid sweetener
¼ cup canola oil, raw nut butter, melted coconut oil or Earth Balance™

1. Mix dry ingredients in a large mixing bowl.
2. Drizzle sweetener and fat over dry mixture. Use a rubber spatula to thoroughly combine.
3. Scoop the granola onto a medium, lightly greased baking tray and spread out into an even layer.
4. Bake uncovered or loosely covered until crispy or lightly browned. At 350°F/177°C, the baking will take less than 1 hour. At 225°F/107°C, bake for 2–2 ½ hours. Even on partly cloudy days when the temperature does not rise above 200°F/93°C, you can bake the granola until dry in 6 hours. Stir periodically for even browning. Do not let it burn.

❈ Pita chips, croutons and bruschetta ❦

Slice fresh pita bread into 6–8 wedges, loaves into ¾-inch cubes or baguettes into thin slices. Drizzle bread with oil or brush on oil with a pastry brush. Toss or sprinkle bread with salt and dried herbs. Arrange in a single layer on a dark baking tray and bake uncovered or loosely covered until lightly brown and crispy, 1 ½–2 hours or more depending on the temperature of the oven.

CHAPTER EIGHTEEN
Solar pasteurization & canning

Solar cookers can be used to pasteurize water, milk and juice, can food in boiling water baths and pressure canners, and even disinfect medical waste and sterilize medical equipment. However, the most popular method of solar canning does not meet USDA canning safety guidelines.

Microbes, pasteurization and canning

Recall the food safety temperature chart in Chapter 3. Pasteurization begins at only 149°F/65°C. Boiling water bath canning heats canned food to the boiling point, which kills all live microbes but not their inactive spores. Boiling water baths can be even be used to disinfect medical waste, reducing, but not completely killing, all live microbes. Pressure canning heats canned food to the sterilization point, destroying all spores. Pressure canners can also be used to sterilize (autoclave) reusable medical equipment.

Pasteurizing water, milk and juice

Pasteurization has turned out to be the major use of solar cookers in poor countries. Solar pasteurization is also a useful emergency technique in highly industrialized countries during electricity blackouts, camping trips and for other needs. While pasteurization happens fastest on sunny days with a box cooker or parabolic reflector, pasteurization can also be done on partly cloudy days even in a simple cardboard panel cooker because the water does not need to reach the boiling point. You heard that right — liquids don't have to actually boil in order to be pasteurized. Water, milk or juice simply needs to be heated in a covered pot at 149°F/65°C for 6 minutes, or to a higher temperature for a shorter time, to kill bacteria, viruses and parasites. Of course, the actual heating time is longer than that, due to the time it takes to heat the water up to the pasteurization temperature.

Several commercial Water Pasteurization Indicators (WAPI) are available that inform you when liquid has been heated to the pasteurization point for a long enough period of time. A WAPI is a sealed polycarbonate tube that contains soybean fat at one end. The fat, which melts at 158°F/70°C, flows to the bottom of the tube when the liquid has been sufficiently heated. Thus one can tell at a glance whether or not water has been pasteurized even after it has cooled. A thin plastic thread allows you to remove the WAPI from the pot without having to stick your fingers in the water (which might recontaminate it). A WAPI can be reused indefinitely. The tube is simply inverted for the next use so that the fat starts out at the top. Special plastic solar water bags like the AquaPak™ are now available which contain a built-in WAPI for easy use, no solar cooker needed.

See www.solarcooking.org/pasteurization/default.htm for an introduction to solar pasteurization and links to scientific articles. The Kerr-Cole Sustainable Living Center has available reprints of journal articles describing the original research done under the aegis of Dr. Robert Metcalf.

USDA canning guidelines
The USDA changed its canning guidelines in 1994 to reflect decades of research into safe canning practices. Download the 1994 edition of the *USDA Complete Guide to Home Canning and Preserving* at the National Center for Home Food Preservation Web site: http://foodsafety.psu.edu/canning-guide.html. Post-1994, the USDA endorses two safe methods of canning:

- **Boiling water bath canning:** Boiling water surrounds the canning jars, transferring heat through convection currents to the jar centers. *This method can only be used for high acid foods* that have a pH of less than 4.6, mainly fruit, tomatoes and fermented and pickled vegetables. Pathogenic microbes like botulinum bacteria, E. coli and salmonella cannot grow and reproduce in highly acidic environments. However, *their spores remain alive.* Low acid and alkaline foods like vegetables and meat should NEVER be canned in a boiling water bath unless their pH is lowered through fermentation (sauerkraut, kimchee) or vinegar pickling.

- **Pressure canning:** Pressure canners reach 250°F/121°C, hot enough to kill the spores of pathogens. Pressure canning is suitable for both high acid and low acid/alkaline foods including vegetables, beans, soups and stews and anything containing animal products.

Parabolic reflectors work just like a stovetop for the purposes of water bath and pressure canning. Follow USDA guidelines as they are written.

The USDA considers the following canning methods either dangerous or untested. Some of these methods could potentially be made safe and effective through further research into minimum canning times for different foods, but right now there are no USDA safe canning guidelines available:

- Oven canning
- Open kettle canning
- Steam canning
- Microwave canning
- Dishwasher canning

Solar boiling water bath canning

You can heat a boiling water bath in a solar box cooker. The drawback to this approach is that it takes a long time for water to heat up to a rolling boil. In my Sun Oven™ it takes several hours to heat a pot of water to boiling, and then the actual processing time is added on top of that. Use a hybrid electric box cooker to maintain an even boiling water bath temperature even if clouds obscure the sun during the middle of a canning run.

Another safe option is to use a box or panel cooker to preheat water for stovetop canning and/or to cook the fruit, tomatoes or jam in a box or panel cooker in preparation for stovetop canning. Both of these methods will save some energy.

The pH scale: high acid foods, low acids foods and alkaline foods

The pH scale measures the acidity or alkalinity of a food or liquid. A pH of less than 7 is acidic. A pH of 7 is neutral. A pH greater than 7 is basic (alkaline). High acid foods have a pH of less than 4.6. High acid environments inhibit the growth of pathogenic microbes and their inactive spores. Low acid and alkaline pH environments, especially oxygenless environments such as the interior of sealed canning jars, allow spores to reactivate.

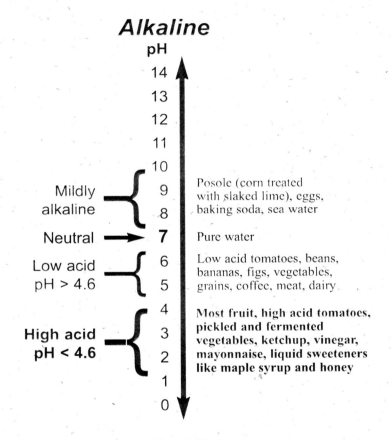

Alkaline
pH

	14	
	13	
	12	
	11	
	10	
Mildly alkaline	9	Posole (corn treated with slaked lime), eggs, baking soda, sea water
	8	
Neutral →	7	Pure water
Low acid pH > 4.6	6	Low acid tomatoes, beans, bananas, figs, vegetables, grains, coffee, meat, dairy
	5	
High acid pH < 4.6	4	**Most fruit, high acid tomatoes, pickled and fermented vegetables, ketchup, vinegar, mayonnaise, liquid sweeteners like maple syrup and honey**
	3	
	2	
	1	
	0	

Acidic

Because it takes such a long time to heat up a boiling water bath in a solar box cooker, the most popular method of solar canning for high acid foods, known as "air canning," skips the water bath and involves placing canning jars filled with fruits or tomatoes directly into a solar box cooker. Unfortunately, this method is similar to oven canning, which as explained above, is rejected by the USDA.

I have had extensive conversations trying to sort out fact from fiction with professors of food science and microbiology, as well as solar cooker inventors such as Barbara Kerr, who was trained as a registered nurse. My conclusion, endorsed by Kerr, is that air canning could potentially be made safe, but right now there is no practical way to assess when a jar of food is fully heated to the center for the correct length of time.

In Kerr's book *The Expanding World of Solar Box Cookers*, she recommends following the USDA boiling water bath canning times for solar air canning. The problem with this recommendation is that convection currents in water transfer heat to a canning jar much more effectively than do convection currents in hot air. Therefore, air-canned foods that are canned using water bath canning times are under-processed. It is important to note that even if a good vacuum seal forms on a canning jar, the food may still contain spoilage organisms like bacteria and mold that can survive in acidic conditions.

Another air canning technique I have come across involves heating the jars until the liquid inside starts to bubble through the canning lid. This method clearly compromises the integrity of the vacuum seal and therefore exposes the food to microbial recontamination from the outside.

Solar cooking advocates who work in poor countries dismiss these concerns. From their point of view, helping people with inadequate food supplies find better ways to store food eclipses the issue of canning spoilage. In August, 2004 I carried on an e-mail correspondence with solar water pasteurization expert and Professor of Microbiology Dr. Robert Metcalf from California State University at Sacramento, and Penn State University Professor of Food Science Dr. Luke LaBorde.

Metcalf, says, "The only problem which might arise with solar canning (of acidic foods), therefore, would be growth of non-pathogens. This is not a public health problem, as C. botulinum won't grow (in acidic foods). I've successfully canned peaches, cherries, applesauce, and jellies using a solar box cooker. If the vacuum seal is in effect after I let the jars cool, there will be no problem. If a seal hasn't been obtained, perhaps a mold spore can get inside the cooled acid food, and eventually grow into a colony. That won't be fun to see, but it will present no public health hazard."

On the other hand, LaBorde says that, "Unlike pathogens, spoilage organisms leave a trail of foul smells, cloudy liquid, fuzzy specks, or general discolorations that evolution has thankfully programmed us to avoid. So it is easy for the consumer to pick out the bad jars and eat from only the wholesome looking ones. However, our understanding of the effects of spoilage organisms on health, particularly with respect to molds, is incomplete. One thing we do know is that spoilage organisms, if allowed to grow can raise the product pH thus creating conditions whereby previously dormant pathogen spores might grow. ...(T)he benefit of increased supplies of food to undernourished people (in developing countries, where Dr. Robert Metcalf does most of his work) far outweighs the slight risk from a few spoiled jars. However, we owe it to them to present all the information so they can make an informed decision. ... When addressing home food preservation questions, I always take the conservative approach and I still cannot recommend any canning procedure that results in an under processed product."

It is possible that someone could use professional food canning research guidelines to test solar air canning and develop a list of safe minimum canning times for different foods and jar sizes that meets the stringency of the USDA canning guidelines. The Washington State University Cooperative Extension Web site says, "The development of a canning recipe is an extensive process. It involves repeating the entire preparation and canning process 15–30 times to obtain accurate heat penetration data. Then, microorganisms are put into the jars before processing to make sure the processing time is sufficient to destroy them. This research must take place in a laboratory with equipment for testing heat penetration and microbiology. This is why processing times cannot be made up!"

An obstacle to developing guidelines for solar air canning is that box cookers vary significantly in terms of their maximum temperature. Guidelines must be based on the temperature of the cooker, which would include the need for very accurate oven thermometers. It would also be necessary to measure the inside of each canning jar with a temperature indicator such as a diack tube, which used to be used in steam pressure autoclaves during the sterilization of medical instruments. Similar to WAPIs, diacks are thick walled glass vials containing a temperature-sensitive pellet which melts when the sterilization temperature has been reached. An attached thread allows the diack to be suspended in a bio-hazard bag filled with water. The trick would be to read the indicator without having to open the canning jar and thus contaminate the contents. Such a procedure might turn out to be more trouble than it's worth.

Solar pressure canning

Pressure canning is easily done in a reflector-only cooker, such as a panel cooker or parabolic reflector. Barbara Kerr and Jim Scott have done extensive experiments with solar pressure canning and sterilization. The experiments are designed to help people in poor countries build similar models from easily available discarded materials.

Kerr has a large panel cooker built out of four 4' x 8' plywood sheets covered with aluminum foil. The panels are used to heat a huge 46-quart All-American Medical Sterilizer (pressure canner) that has been painted black. The sterilizer has an emergency metal/spring or neoprene disk for safety pressure release. Metal disks that melt as an over-pressure safety release do not work since they melt prematurely from the solar heat that falls on the top of the vessel. For insulation, a chicken wire cage is wrapped around the canner, leaving an air gap for insulation. A sheet of plastic, such as a discarded piece of mattress wrapping, is wrapped around the chicken wire cage to act as a giant cooking bag. The trick is maintaining the right balance of heat retention and venting so that the canner remains at high pressure throughout the canning period. Because pressure canners have both a temperature gauge and visible vent steam, it is easy to see when the temperature and pressure is correct.

Most importantly, the system has a back-up propane heater designed to kick in if clouds obscure the sun during the middle of a canning run. In order for the contents to be safely sterilized, the pressure must not be allowed to drop.

See the article, "The Kerr-Cole Large Solar Panel/Propane Hybrid Stoves" at http://solarcooking.org/ hybrid-propane.htm.

Kerr-Cole Large Solar Panel/Propane Hybrid Stove
NOT SHOWN: underneath the bottom panel is a backup propane stove.

Medical disinfection and sterilization

Using solar cookers to disinfect infectious biomedical waste and even sterilize (autoclave) medical equipment is the next frontier in poor countries. Maybe someday these techniques will be used in the United States, too.

Solar box cookers are very reliable at killing microbes in a water bath. For example, a study published in the Oct. 18, 2003 issue of *The Lancet* used a single reflector box cooker with a backup electric heating element in case of clouds. Infectious waste such as bandages and simulated waste inoculated with specific pathogenic bacteria was immersed in a water bath that ranged from 68° C to 87° C (154.4° F to 190.4° F) from 10 a.m. to 4 p.m. The cooker was reoriented towards the sun every 2 to 3 hours. The study reports that the process creates a 7-log reduction in bacteria. "(A)fter solar heat exposure we could not detect any surviving bacteria (detection threshold 10 bacteria per mL)," even though samples included "very high loads" of "multiple drug resistant bacteria." Following treatment in the solar cooker, the waste can be safely disposed of without fear of spreading disease. See a summary written for non-scientists at http://solarcooking.org/research/Medical_Waste-Chitnis.pdf.

Barbara Kerr's solar pressure canner can also be used as an autoclave to sterilize medical equipment for reuse. Again, when used properly, pressure canners kill all pathogenic spores. The system has a backup propane heating tank in case clouds appear during the middle of a firing. See the article, "Use of the Solar Panel Cooker for Medical Pressure Steam Sterilization at http://solarcooking.org/bkerr/AutoclaveEditMay2006_pdfe.pdf.

CHAPTER NINETEEN

Make ice & cool food with your solar cooker!

o you live in a dry climate and have a multiple reflector oven or funnel cooker? Double its usefulness by using it at night as a radiant cooler to cool food and make ice. The reflectors will reflect infrared radiation (heat) from the food or water into the night sky, which acts as a heat sink.

- In humid climates, moisture in the atmosphere acts as an insulating blanket that prevents efficient radiant cooling.
- The atmosphere must be clear and calm. Clouds act as insulating blankets while wind stirs up warmer and cooler atmospheric layers, creating warmer temperatures near the ground.
- Place the cooker in a location that has the fullest possible exposure to the night sky. Keep the cooker away from buildings, trees, boulders and other objects (thermal masses) that radiate heat into the air.
- Remove the cooker's glass or plastic glazing.
- Place the food or water in the cooker in an open container. If desired, cover the container with an ordinary polyethylene supermarket produce bag, which allows infrared radiation to pass through unobstructed.
- To freeze water or juice, pour no more than ½ inch into a dark, lidless pot, pan or ice cube tray.
- Food and water can be cooled up to 20°F/36°C below the minimum ambient air temperature. Water freezes in the right weather conditions when the minimum temperature drops to 52°F/11°C or below.
- In the morning before the sun rises, transfer the food or ice to a cooler or ice chest to keep food cool.

PART III
The sustainable kitchen

On cloudy days, I switch to two other
environmentally-friendly, energy-saving cooking
methods: fireless cooking and pressure cooking.
Fireless cookers are insulated boxes.
Food is brought to a boil on a stovetop,
simmered briefly, then placed in
the fireless cooker to finish cooking using
the retained heat. Pressure cookers have very
tight lids to lock in heated steam, which raises
the pressure, and thus the temperature,
of the cooking pot to 250°F/121°C.

Solar, fireless and pressure cookers
work well in conjunction with one another.
Solar cookers can be used to heat a cooking pot
that will be placed in a fireless cooker.
Pressure cookers make great pots for
fireless cookers because of their tight lids.
By combining these three cooking methods
with a biomass-fueled cooking method,
it is possible to create a year-round
sustainable cooking system.

CHAPTER TWENTY
Fireless cooking

A fireless cooker is an insulated box that retains the heat of a cooking pot, allowing the food to finish cooking without additional heat. Solar and slow cooker recipes are easily adjusted to fireless cooking since all three involve slow cooking at low to moderate temperatures.

A brief history of fireless cooking

For hundreds of years, European peasants stuffed wooden boxes with hay. Often, the boxes would serve double use as benches and include elaborate carvings and decorations. During World War I and II, hay boxes helped people survive fuel rationing. Early electric and gas ovens were equipped with

automatic shut-offs and lots of insulation so they could conveniently be used as all-in-one fireless cookers. In England during World War II, fireless cookers were known as "Victory Ovens," companions to Victory Gardens. Today, peak oil and global warming are renewing interest in fireless cooking.

Make your own fireless cooker

A fireless cooker can be made of many different materials. The simplest choice for many is to use a commercial cooler. The insulation meant to keep food cold is just as good at keeping food hot! My fireless cooker is a mid-sized Coleman™ cooler filled with old blankets. The cooler is also used as a bench in my kitchen. Another idea is to use two nested cardboard boxes with insulation material in between them. Even something as simple as a large basket can work as an outer container.

- A fireless cooker must be large enough to contain at least 4 inches of insulation on all six sides of the largest pot you plan to use in the cooker.
- The box must be airtight to prevent the escape of heat.
- Cover the inner surfaces of the box with heat-reflective material like foil (This step is not necessary if using a commercial cooler).
- Leave enough room to accommodate a 2-quart or larger cooking pot as desired. Pots smaller than 2-quarts do not retain enough heat to make the fireless cooking process work.
- Tuck loose insulation such as old blankets or sleeping bags around the pot.

Solar cookers can also be used as fireless cookers; once the food has been brought to a boil and simmered for at least the minimum of time, stuff insulation pillows directly around the cooking pot and close the reflectors. By this means one can continue cooking in a solar oven when clouds roll in. Swaddling the cooker with a quilt will extend the heat retention time.

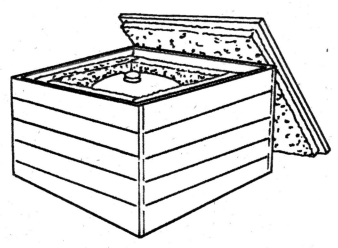

Using a fireless cooker

Fireless cooking can be used to cook any food that is simmered, pressure cooked, steamed or poached in liquid, including grains, polenta, beans, stews, root vegetables, fruit compote and steamed breads. Fireless cooking saves between one-third and 95 percent of the fuel that would otherwise be needed to cook the food.

The fireless cooking process has two parts: *simmering time* and *cooker time*. First the food must be brought to a boil on the stovetop or in a solar cooker. Once the food has begun to boil, it is simmered for a short period of time, ranging from 2–20 minutes depending on the type of food, to allow the heat to penetrate to the center of each individual piece of food. Then the pot is transferred to the fireless cooker. Fireless cookers retain enough heat to stay above the microbial danger zone (above 140°F/60°C) for up to four hours.

- Fireless cooking times are 2–3 times longer than conventional simmering.
- Because food cooks at an ever-decreasing temperature, it will not burn. The fireless cooker time is quite flexible, beyond the bare minimum.
- Pots must have a tight-fitting lid to adequately retain the cooking heat. While regular saucepans and stock pots can be used in a fireless cooker, a pressure cooker is ideal. Pressure cookers do not have to be brought to high pressure (although that will lower the cooking time); to use like a regular pot, simmer without the vent cover and add vent cover just before placing pot in the fireless cooker. Heavy pots made out of cast iron, such as Dutch ovens, or stainless steel or aluminum pressure cookers, retain heat more effectively than thin-walled pots such as enameled graniteware.
- The smallest volume of food that will retain enough heat in a fireless cooker is 2 ½–3 cups, such as 1 cup grain in 2 cups water. Longer-cooking foods like dry beans require at least twice that volume to cook properly. Water's properties as a thermal mass is what holds the heat during the cooking process.
- Fill the cooking pot about 2/3 full with the food and cooking water. Allow about two inches of space at the top of the pot for steam buildup.
- Food requires less water than it would need if cooked on a conventional stovetop or oven because moisture is sealed inside the pot. Similarly, less spice in needed because the aroma does not boil away into the air.
- Large foods like winter squashes should be chopped into smaller pieces. When cooking quicker-cooking foods together with longer cooking foods, for example, stewing carrots with lentils, leave the quicker-cooking foods in larger pieces so that the different foods will be finished cooking, but not overcooked, at the same time.
- To experiment with new dishes, make a reasonable guess for the simmering and fireless cooker times. If the food is undercooked, simmer on the stovetop until done and adjust the times for next time.

- If you are running out of meal preparation time, the food can simply be simmered for a longer time before being placed in the fireless cooker to shorten the fireless cooker time.
- The cooker must be kept tightly closed until the food is finished cooking in order to retain adequate heat. No peeking!
- Foods that have been left in a fireless cooker for more than four hours should be reheated to boiling before serving. Food left longer than 12 hours should be discarded.
- After a cooking pot has been removed from your fireless cooker, allow the cooking box and insulation materials to air out so that no moisture remains trapped in the cooker. Periodically wipe out the box and wash or replace the insulation materials when they begin to retain cooking odors.

Fireless cooker recipes

Because I live at 7,000 feet altitude where the boiling point is only 199°F/93°C, everything takes longer to cook than it does at sea level. The following cooking times are for 1) sea level cooking in a regular pot or 2) high altitude cooking in a pressure cooker. My testing shows that at my altitude, fireless cooking times in a pressure cooker are exactly the same as that for a non-pressure cooker at sea level. If you use a pressure cooker at sea level, cut down on both simmering and fireless cooker time.

❋ Soup stock ❋

To make 4 quarts broth use a 6-quart pot. Simmer 15 minutes and place in the fireless cooker for 3–4 hours.

❋ Fireless stew ❋

Your favorite soup, stew and tomato sauce recipes can be easily adapted to fireless cooking. Simply follow a recipe's conventional cooking directions until it says to turn down the temperature and simmer. When using my pressure cooker, I cook the stew at full pressure for 1–2 minutes, and then transfer the pot to the fireless cooker for 1 hour. If using a standard 4-quart soup pot, simmer stew for 15 minutes. Transfer pot to fireless cooker and cook for 1 ½ times the length of time required in the original recipe. For example, if a conventional stew recipe says to simmer for 1–2 hours, let it cook in the fireless cooker for 2–3 hours.

❋ Fireless grains and beans ❋

The slow cooking time and low temperatures of fireless cookers create especially fluffy grain dishes and soft beans.

	Simmering time:	Fireless time:
Barley, pearled	5 minutes	1 hour
Buckwheat	3 minutes	30 minutes
Oat groats	4 minutes	1 hour
Posole, presoaked	20 minutes	4 hours
Quinoa	3 minutes	10 minutes
Rice, brown	5 minutes	1 hour
Rice, white	3 minutes	45 minutes
Wheat berries	10 minutes	3 hours
Lentils, unsoaked:	5 minutes	1 hour
Most beans, presoaked:	10 minutes	2 hours
Garbanzos, presoaked:	15 minutes	2 hours

❋ Fireless polenta ❋

Cook polenta in a regular pot, never at high pressure; it can clog the vent. Simmer 5 min. Cook in fireless cooker 1 hour.

❋ Soup dumplings ❋

For large dumplings 1 ½ + inches in diameter, such as matzo balls, simmer 5 minutes and place in fireless cooker 2–3 hours. Small dumplings get mushy in a fireless cooker.

❋ Whole potatoes ❋

To cook whole potatoes, use a minimum of 5 cups of water to hold sufficient heat. In a 2–3 quart pot, partially or wholly submerge 4–6 potatoes in cold water. The pot should be about two-thirds full with the combination of water and potatoes. Cover, bring to a boil and simmer 5 minutes. Place in fireless cooker 2 ½ hours.

❋ Winter squash ❦

Chop several cups of winter squash into 1–2 inch pieces.
Partially submerge in water or broth. Simmer 6 minutes and
cook in fireless cooker 2 hours.

❋ Glazed root vegetables ❦

Use the glazed root vegetable recipe in Chapter Thirteen, but
double for greater thermal mass. Simmer 5 minutes and leave
in fireless cooker 2 hours.

❋ Steamed breads and cakes ❦

Yeast breads, quick breads and cakes are all steamed the same
way. Read the solar steamed breads instructions in Chapter
Sixteen. I use an enameled graniteware roaster I found at an
antique store that fits perfectly around a 1-quart bundt pan.
Use 5 cups water to partially surround the mold or several
smaller cans. Raise the top of the mold at least 1 inch above
the water. Bring the water to a rolling boil, and then lower
into covered mold. Simmer 30 minutes. If you are at high altitude, simmer 45 minutes. Cook in fireless cooker 4 hours.

❋ Incubating yogurt ❦

A fireless cooker is a perfect place to incubate yogurt. Heat a
pot of water to incubation temperature (108–112°F/42–44°C),
submerge a jar of inoculated milk, cover and place in fireless
cooker several hours, until yogurt is thick.

CHAPTER TWENTY ONE
Pressure cooking

pressure cooker should be a staple appliance in every sustainable kitchen, especially at high altitude. If you are not already a fan of pressure cooking, I hope to convince you to become one. If you already have a pressure cooker, I will show you some new ways to use it as part of a sustainable kitchen.

Super fast, super efficient, super safe

By raising the temperature of boiling food to a superheated 250°F/121°C and sealing in the heat with a super tight lid, pressure cookers lower fuel use on an ordinary stovetop by a whopping 75 percent or more. Cooking takes only 10–50 percent as long as with a regular saucepan. Modern pressure cookers, unlike their antique cousins, are designed to be very safe. They have a locking lid with a rubber gasket and a lever locking mechanism on the handle to hold in high pressures safely. The rubber gasket is a circular seal around the edge of the cooker lid. A steam vent regulates the pressure level inside the cooker and an emergency release valve prevents dangerous buildups of steam if the steam vent clogs or malfunctions.

Pressure cookers can be used to cook any food that is boiled or steamed, including grains, polenta, legumes, meats, vegetables, stews, fruit preserves and steamed breads. If you want to cook your own beans and whole grains, a pressure cooker greatly reduces the. Even small-sized pastas like orzo or rotelli can be cooked in a pressure cooker. Because the food cooks so quickly, whole vegetables hold their shape, color and vitamins better than conventional cooking methods. The flavors of soups and stews intermingle so well that a 4-minute stew tastes like it has simmered for hours.

Using a pressure cooker in a solar cooker

Using a pressure cooker with a parabolic reflector is as easy as on a stovetop. See Chapter Eighteen for Barbara Kerr's experiments with heating a 46-quart pressure canner with a large solar panel cooker.

Pressure cookers can also be used in solar box and panel cookers. Some pressure cookers have a plastic or metal safety plug that melts if the temperature goes too far above 250°F/121°C, allowing the pressure to be released. Silicone safety valves have a much higher melting point. To prevent a plastic or metal safety plug from overheating, try shading the plug with a small piece of aluminum foil; the foil can be tacked in place with small dabs of silicone on the corners. To help regulate the pressure inside the pressure cooker, turn the solar cooker away from the sun if the pressure cooker appears to be releasing too much steam — an indication that the pressure is too high.

Choosing a pressure cooker

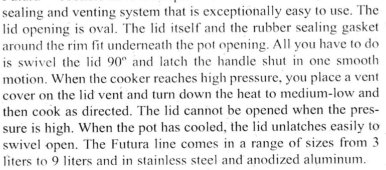

When choosing a pressure cooker, make sure it is sized properly for your family's needs. Pressure cookers cannot be filled more than ½–2/3 full.

My pressure cooker is a dark gray 3-liter Hawkins-Futura™. Hawkins-Futura™ cookers have a unique sealing and venting system that is exceptionally easy to use. The lid opening is oval. The lid itself and the rubber sealing gasket around the rim fit underneath the pot opening. All you have to do is swivel the lid 90° and latch the handle shut in one smooth motion. When the cooker reaches high pressure, you place a vent cover on the lid vent and turn down the heat to medium-low and then cook as directed. The lid cannot be opened when the pressure is high. When the pot has cooled, the lid unlatches easily to swivel open. The Futura line comes in a range of sizes from 3 liters to 9 liters and in stainless steel and anodized aluminum.

CHAPTER TWENTY TWO

Earth ovens

Earth ovens are beehive-shaped, wood burning ovens made of earth, clay, sand and straw. These primitive masonry ovens can be easily built out of cheap, locally available materials by relatively unskilled people. Earth ovens cook by radiant heat, excellent for baking pizza, artisan breads, roasted foods and casseroles.

Earth, clay, sand and straw

Earth ovens are made with cob, a clay-like mixture of earth, clay, sand and straw. The mixture can also be dried first into adobe bricks, like the adobe *hornos* (ovens) introduced into Pueblo villages in the American Southwest by Spanish settlers. Earthen and lime plasters are used to coat the outer surface. Earth ovens can be built on the ground or on a platform constructed out of rocks, bricks, "urbanite" (broken slabs of concrete) or wood. An oven can even be built on a trailer. *Build Your Own Earth Oven*, by Kiko Denzer, details the entire process from building the oven to baking sourdough bread.

The most basic earth ovens have one chamber, with or without a chimney. A fire is built in the oven chamber itself and must burn for at least an hour or more to heat up the earthen mass of the oven. Earth ovens burn scrap wood, making good use of cast off resources. The most important skill required is learning how to build and maintain a proper fire — small but hot. The ashes are raked out and the food is inserted. Two-chamber designs separate the wood-burning chamber from the food chamber for continual heat.

The neighborhood bread oven

Before the Industrial Revolution led many people to abandon home bread baking, European villages often had a single shared earth oven cared for by the village baker. Because fuelwood was often scarce, firing would only happen once a week. Housewives would make their own dough and bring their loaves to the oven on baking day slashed with a distinctive branding pattern to distinguish her loaves from everyone else's. Today, the growing popularity of earth ovens is reviving the idea of the neighborhood bread oven. An earth oven workshop is a great neighborhood project for all ages. I helped to build an earth oven in a community garden. In addition, I have a friend who held an earth oven workshop in his backyard.

Those of us who are aficionados of artisan bread agree that no other bread compares to artisan loaves baked directly on the hearth of a traditional wood fired earth or masonry oven. Heat radiates from all sides of the interior, producing extraordinary oven spring and a thick, crunchy crust. A fully heated oven will reach 600–700°F/316–371°C, perfect for four-minute pizzas and flatbreads. As the oven cools down, it becomes suitable for other types of bread, as well as casseroles, roasted foods, and much more. As the temperature drops, the remaining heat can be used to incubate yogurt and dry food.

"Wherever there is a tradition of baking bread in a wood-fired oven, there is also a host of other traditional foods, from slow-cooked casseroles to baked vegetables, that make use of the oven's waning heat," say Jeffrey Alford and Naomi Duguid in their book *Flatbreads & Flavors.*

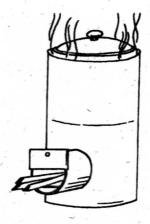

CHAPTER TWENTY THREE

Biomass stoves

If you have a cast iron woodstove, you already have a sustainable backup stove. If not, a small, super-efficient wood-fired stove like the Aprovecho rocket stove makes an excellent back-up stove burner. The rocket stove is a one-burner stove made from inexpensive materials like used tin cans and old sections of stovepipe.

Energy efficent biomass cooking

Dr. Larry Winiarski, a researcher with the nonprofit Aprovecho Research Institute, invented the rocket stove. The stove has thick insulation around the combustion chamber and chimney, which keeps the fire above 1,100°F/593°C, for nearly complete combustion and reducing smoke, which is composed of unburned particles of soot and gas. The cooking pot sits atop the chimney, in contact with the flame, for efficient heat transfer. The pot is insulated by a metal skirt. The Aprovecho Web site says, "Rocket stoves use branches, twigs, small wood scraps, or just about any small combustible material. The pieces of wood or other material burn at their tips, increasing combustion efficiency." The rocket bread oven funnels the heat up through an insulated 55-gallon drum for energy efficient baking.

Aprovecho's booklet, *Capturing Heat I: Five Earth-Friendly Technologies and How to Build Them* provides instructions for building these designs. Another good resource for information on rocket stoves is the article, "Cooking Fuel Conservation — A Guide to Stovetop Food Heating Efficiency," from the Kerr-Cole Sustainable Living Center.

PART IV

Sustainable cooking resources

Web sites, books, CD-Roms, DVDs and nonprofit organizations to help you transition to a sustainable way of cooking.

APPENDIX

Sustainable cooking resources

Solar cooking conference proceedings, nonprofit organizations & Web sites

Kerr-Cole Sustainable Living Center, http://solarcooking.org/bkerr/, kerrcole@frontiernet.net, P.O. Box 576, Taylor, AZ 85939, Physical address: 3310 Paper Mill Road in Taylor, Tel: 928-536-226.

Solar Cookers International, www.solarcookers.org, info@solarcookers.org, 1919 21st St., #101, Sacramento, CA 95811-6827, 916-455-4499. Publisher of *Solar Cooker Review* journal. Sponsor of the Solar Cooking Archive and Solar Cooking Wiki.

Solar Cooking Archive, www.solarcooking.org. Plans, recipes, research, blogs, international reports, and more.

Solar Cooking Wiki, http://solarcooking.wikia.com/wiki/Main_Page.

Solar Cookers and Food Processing 2006 International Conference. CD-Rom. Sponsored by SCI and Terra Foundation. Posters and papers.

Solar cookbooks

Cooking With Sunshine, by Lorraine Anderson and Rick Palkovic, Marlow & Company, 1994, 2006. Non-vegetarian.

The Expanding World of Solar Box Cookers, Barbara Prosser Kerr, 1991. Available for free download at www.solarcooking.org/kerr.htm. The most complete resource for single reflector box cookers.

Eleanor's Solar Cookbook,Eleanor Shimeall, 1983. Cemese Publishers, P.O. Box 1022, Borrego Springs, CA 92004. 93 pp. Recipes for single reflector box cookers. Canning instructions do not meet USDA guidelines.

Heaven's Flame, Joseph M. Radabaugh, Home Power Publishing, 1998. 143 pp. This is the book you need if you want to design and build your own cookers (above and beyond following someone else's plan).

Solar Cooking, Harriet Kofalk, Book Publishing Company, 1995. 96 pp. Vegan recipes for single reflector box cookers.

The Morning Hill Solar Cookery Book, Jennifer Barker, Morning Hill Associates, 1999, 100 pp., www.highdesertnet.com/morninghill/solar cook.htm. The cook lives in Oregon. Vegetarian recipes tested in a Sun Oven'". Some vegan recipes. Vague cooking times (i.e. "cook until done").

The Solar Chef Cookbook, self-published by Solar Ranch, www.solar-ranch.com. 75 Southwestern recipes tested in a Sun Oven™ in New Mexico. Non-vegetarian.

The Solar Cookery Book, Beth and Dan Halacy, Morning Sun Press, 1992, 114 pp. The Halacy's have been using solar cookers of all kinds for more than 40 years. The recipes are designed for both box cookers and parabolic reflectors. Includes plans for building a plywood multi-reflector box cooker, a cardboard one-panel box cooker, and a cardboard parabolic reflector. Non-vegetarian.

Solar Cooking Naturally, Virginia Heather Gurley, Sunlight Works Inc.,1993. 92 pp. Single reflector box cooker recipes tested in Sedona, Arizona. Includes a few vegetarian entrees.

Vegetarian slow cooking

125 Best Vegetarian Slow Cooker Recipes, Judith Finlayson, Robert Rose, 2004. 192 pp.

Fast Cooking in a Slow Cooker Every Day of the Year, Joann Rachor, Family Health Publications, 2005. 144 pp.

Fresh from the Vegetarian Slow Cooker, Robin Robertson, Harvard Common Press, 2004. 288 pp.

Real Food Vegetarian Recipes For Your Slo-Cooker, Annette Yates (Editor), Foulsham, 2004. 144 pp.

The Simple Little Vegan Slow Cooker, Michelle A. Rivera, Book Publishing Company, 2005. 127 pp.

The Vegetarian Slow Cooker, Joanna White, Nitty Gritty Cookbooks, Bristol Publishing Enterprises, 2001. 160 pp.

Solar food drying

A solar food dryer that really works, Larisa Walk, Countryside & Small Stock Journal, 2000. Available for download at www.Amazon.com.

The Solar Food Dryer: How to Make and Use Your Own Low-Cost, High Performance, Sun-Powered Food Dehydrator, Eben V. Fodor, New Society Publishers, 2006. 144 pp. Plans and instructions for using a direct sunlight dryer designed by Fodor.

Solar Food Dryers Web page, www.solarcooking.org/drying/default.htm.

Food safety, water pasteurization, canning & sterilization

Water Pasteurization Indicator, http://solarcookers.org/order/order.html

A Summary of Water Pasteurization Techniques, http://solarcooking.org/solarwat.htm

The Microbiology of Solar Cooking, Marshall Logvin, Master's Thesis, 1980, California State University, Sacramento. Call the university library and they'll make a photocopy for you for a small fee.

Box cooker biomedical disinfection summary, http://solarcooking.org/research/Medical_Waste-Chitnis.pdf.

Use of the solar panel cooker for medical pressure steam sterilization, www.solarcooking.org/bkerr/AutoclaveEditMay2006_ pdfe.pdf.

USDA Complete Guide to Home Canning, http://foodsafety.psu.edu/canningguide.html, 1994.

Using your solar cooker to cool food & make ice

How to Use the Solar Funnel as a Refrigerator/ Cooler, http://solarcooking.org/funnel.htm.

Using a Solar Oven as a Radiant Refrigerator at Night, http://solarcooking.org/radiant-fridge.htm.

Sustainable cooking

Aprovecho Research Center, www.aprovecho.net. Non-profit research and education about Appropriate Technology, Sustainable Forestry, Organic Agriculture and Permaculture. *Capturing Heat I* has step-by-step instructions on how to build a rocket stove, a rocket bread oven, a fireless cooker, a multiple reflector solar box cooker and a parabolic reflector. *Capturing Heat II* includes plans for fuel-efficient cooking stoves with chimneys, a pizza/bread oven, and solar and wood-fired hot water heaters.

Cooking Fuel Conservation — A Guide to Stovetop Food Heating Efficiency, Kerr-Cole Sustainable Living Center, http://www.solarcooking.org/bkerr/FuelConserve-0d.pdf. *The Post-Petroleum Survival Guide and Cookbook*, Albert K. Bates, New Society Publishers, 2006. 236 pp.

The Sustainable Kitchen, Barbara Kerr, 1991, http://solarcooking.org/sustainable-kitchen.htm.

Fireless cooking

Cooking Without Fuel, Julia Older, Yankee Books, 1982. 80 pp.

Fireless Cookery, Heidi Kirschner, Madrona Publishers, 1981. 179 pp.

The Fireless Cookbook, Margaret J. Mitchell, 1909, reprinted in 2006 by Creative Cookbooks. 328 pp. Old-fashioned recipes.

Heat-Retention Cooking, www.solarcooking.org/heat%2Dretention.

What is fireless cooking?, http://community-2.webtv.net/adowning/FirelessCooking.

Pressure cooking

Great Vegetarian Cooking Under Pressure, Lorna J. Sass, Morrow Cookbooks, 1994. 288 pp.

Hawkins-Futura pressure cookers, www.baycityintl.com.

Wood burning stoves & earth ovens

BioEnergy Lists: Biomass Cooking Stoves, www.bioenergylists.org.

Build Your Own Earth Oven, Kiko Denzer, Hand Print Press, 3rd edition, 2007. 132 pp.

Kiko Denzer's Web site, www.intabas.com/kikodenzer.htm

Earth-mud-cob-adobe-horno-oven-links, http://handyprojects.blogspot.com/2005/04/earth-mud-cob-adobe-horno-oven-links.html

Illustrations

Acknowledgments

Special thanks to Zackery Zdinack for the drawings of solar cookers. Life Drawing & Education, P.O. Box 1314, Flagstaff, AZ 86002, www.lifedraw.com, wildlife@lifedraw.com.

For technical assistance, recipe testing and proof reading: Amber Faith, Dan Frazier, Barbara Kerr, Nancy Maurer, Marlene and Dennis Rayner, Jim Scott, Allison Weber.

Lee Vadnais, for inventing the title "The Sunny Side of Cooking" for my Coconino Community College solar cooking workshops.

Dr. Diane Herson, Dr. Luke LaBorde and Dr. Robert Metcalf for information on the microbiology of solar cooking and canning.

My husband, Dan Frazier, for eating the food I cook and keeping my kitchen clean.

My cat, Garfunkel, 1991–2007, and my new kittens Pablo and Sasha for keeping me company while I wrote this book.

About the author

The daughter of a chemist and a biologist, Lisa Rayner has long had an interest in the natural world. As a young girl she was an avid sea shell collector. She spent much of her time exploring the forest around her Delaware home.

Lisa hated cooking growing up. Then, in 1985 she became vegetarian, and soon after, vegan. She spent the next year-and-a-half teaching herself to cook and in the process discovered she enjoyed it. In 1993 she was in the middle of teaching a six-week vegetarian cooking class when she realized that what she really wanted to learn about was which foods grew in her cool, dry mountain home. She began to learn all she could about both growing and cooking bioregionally-appropriate foods. In 1996 Lisa obtained a word processor while dumpster-diving and subsequently wrote *Growing Food in the Southwest Mountains: A Permaculture Approach to Gardening Above 6,500 Feet*. She published the 3rd edition of the book in 2002.

Lisa has a Bachelor of Science degree in Natural Resource Interpretation from Northern Arizona University. She is a graduate of the 1993 Black Mesa Permaculture Project's design certification course.

Lisa lives with her husband Dan Frazier in Flagstaff, Arizona. She teaches sustainable cooking and permaculture workshops in northern Arizona. She is currently working on several cookbooks with bioregional, vegan and sustainable themes.